Praise for The Green Budget Guide

'This is wonderful. The planet and we need more Nancy! This book is so accessible and it reads as she speaks and it does as she does. It's worth its weight in gold and so is Nancy.'

Gaby Roslin, broadcaster and author of *Spread the Joy*

'What a wonderful pick and mix of tips and tricks. Nancy has done it again! Since Nancy told me to use cereal packet liners, I haven't bought a single roll of cling film so I am excited to dive into all these hacks and tricks to save even more pennies. The five minute veg stock is RIGHT up my street! The win here is two-fold because it's great for the pocket and the planet so we all win. I keep my other Nancy books in my utility because that is often where I am when I think "What would Nancy do?" and this one will certainly be joining that collection and undoubtedly become as well-loved as the others.'

Daisy Upton, author of *Five Minute Mum*

The Green Budget Guide

101 Planet and Money Saving Tips,
Ideas and Recipes

NANCY BIRTWHISTLE

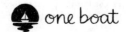
one boat

First published 2024 by One Boat
an imprint of Pan Macmillan
The Smithson, 6 Briset Street, London EC1M 5NR
EU representative: Macmillan Publishers Ireland Ltd, 1st Floor,
The Liffey Trust Centre, 117–126 Sheriff Street Upper,
Dublin 1, D01 YC43
Associated companies throughout the world
www.panmacmillan.com

ISBN 978-1-0350-2673-9

3 5 7 9 10 8 6 4 2

A CIP catalogue record for this book is available from the British Library.

Illustrations by Ruth Craddock

Typeset in Caslon Pro by Palimpsest Book Production Ltd, Falkirk, Stirlingshire
Printed and bound by LSC Communications.

This book contains the opinions and ideas of the author. It is intended to provide helpful
general information on the subjects that it addresses. Before following any instructions
outlined in this book, it is suggested that the reader undertakes a patch test to ensure
suitability and follows any relevant manufacturer or supplier guidelines. The publisher and
author disclaim all responsibility for damage, loss or injury of any kind resulting from tips
or instructions contained in this book. Handle materials with care. For use under
responsible adult supervision only. All necessary precautions should be taken.

Visit **www.panmacmillan.com/bluebird** to read more about all our books
and to buy them. You will also find features, author interviews and
news of any author events, and you can sign up for e-newsletters
so that you're always first to hear about our new releases.

To Tim – thanks for being there.

Contents

Introduction

Whatever anyone's circumstances and whatever is going on politically, every now and then we can feel the pinch a little more than usual. You know the saying, 'it never rains but it pours', and that feeling of 'is there anything else that is going to go wrong?' Once you know that there are many small problems that you can sort out yourself – tricks that cut corners, save energy, repair rather than replace – then the big things that are going to cost money hopefully will not be such a challenge.

When I look back over my many past decades, I can see many times when I had to make tough decisions about how I spent my money. Way back into my teens I never quite had sufficient funds to do what I wanted to do – which was simply to go out, have fun and buy new clothes. So to make the money go further I decided to make my own clothes. Moving on then to the 1970s – me in my twenties, newly married and with a home to run – I had to learn fairly quickly how to manage on a tight budget. Along came children and extra mouths to feed, so I needed to supplement that budget by taking a small, low-paid job, in addition to making clothes in the evenings, baking, cooking and keeping an eye on the utility bills.

Only now do I understand how resourceful those years have made me. I may now have sufficient funds to loosen some of those purse strings, but I find it near on impossible to do so. I am very much set in my ways – I cannot waste food, I will not pay someone to do what I can easily do myself, and there is something very satisfying about achieving a result without having to spend a fortune.

Is it really possible to live a greener lifestyle when every day there may be yet another pressure on our household budget? I am sure each and every one of us has a conscience about the plight of our planet and wants to do our best to live a more sustainable lifestyle; however, the reality is that the tangible pressures of increasing fuel and energy costs have a knock-on effect on other prices across the board, including our food, clothing, renewals, services. In fact, everything.

Let us try not to feel oppressed, overwhelmed or defeated, though. Instead we should think about the crunch areas that have the largest impact on our own daily living – running our homes – and that consequently go on to make us feel the most hard up. Once we have identified these hot spots we can then try to deliver on smarter money-saving methods while still maintaining and hopefully improving our green lifestyle, which in my experience is going to be cheaper and even easier.

Like many people, I am feeling challenged by the increasing cost of living, but am insistent I'll not face these issues in a negative way. I try to critically question and examine the way I do things because then I am also inspired and fired-up, finding myself becoming determined to ride the wave rather than be consumed by it. I honestly believe there are many tips and hacks, smart swaps and clever approaches that we can apply to our daily living that maybe hadn't occurred to us before, and once they become part of our everyday habits, we will wonder why we hadn't always done things this way or that.

Previous generations were very good at being 'budget-friendly' long before 'eco-friendly' became everyday speak, so by combining the two lifestyles we can begin to hit the difficult times with gusto, rising to face the financial challenges, and actually feel quite proud, empowered, resilient and resourceful. I for one know that I will not revert to some of those less price-conscious, throwaway habits that have been costly both on our limited budget and our precious planet.

There will be those who are fortunate enough to not have to juggle a squeezed budget but still want to do their best for the planet and make some everyday changes. Why spend money on something when an easy switch or saving can be made that will free up funds to use on other things? Even though money may not be an issue for everyone, better use of the Earth's valuable finite resources should be on the agenda for all.

My green journey continues at a pace as my eagerness, knowledge and understanding of what I want to achieve become ever clearer. I see for myself from readers who, via social media channels, share their own 'before and after' green success stories that the appetite for living a greener life is increasing, and that people are realizing there is an utter joy in saving money while they're at it. What's not to like? I have a conscience that gets bigger by the day, and if I can do just one thing that day that I know improves on my energy consumption and makes a budget-saving choice, that manages to do two things for the price of one and helps others to do the same – all of that kind of thing – then I am absolutely delighted and in my own small way can feel quite smug knowing I am making a tiny difference to my purse and our planet.

ABOUT THE BOOK

I have divided this book into handy sections and, by the way, I am not relying on anyone having to go out to purchase expensive gadgets or products that promise to save energy, money or the like. I will not be spending on items that I think I need or want in order to save money; my *Green Budget Guide* works with what I already have. With this in mind, I am hoping that you find within this book a box of tools to help you do what you already do but in a more cost-conscious and green way. I have also included a number of thrifty everyday recipes and given them the 'Flexi' title, meaning that they will work with whatever appliances you already have in your kitchen, including the microwave.

I love tricks that avoid waste or mean that those things that are staring us in the face and that we probably hadn't considered could be upcycled to use in a different way – thereby saving pounds, not pennies. It is no secret that I have been around the block a few times, so I have introduced tips from my youth that are more than helpful today as we endeavour to eliminate food waste, save on the household budget and, with little extra effort, are in turn helping our planet.

I understand because I have experienced how it is to have literally no wriggle room within the family budget, and for young families now, I believe it is even harder. I recall a time when just about every penny was taken care of and there was nothing left at the end of the month. I used to laugh to myself when there was talk of 'save a bit and spend a bit'. Savings? How was I ever going to have savings? I survived and am grateful for that experience because it made me capable, and I am here to reassure you that even though times may be tough and different from when I was going through it, you can do the same too.

Whether you want to save money at home, conserve energy usage, work smarter when cooking in the kitchen, get savvy with even the most difficult of stains that have appeared on the laundry, or discover ways to deal with the inevitable everyday household accidents, problems and tasks; whether you are on the move in the car or on public transport; or find yourself stuck for affordable gift ideas – there's something for everyone in this book.

I have included chapter headings that I believe help the reader to navigate this not so little book and have tried within it to answer the many regular questions that I am asked time and again. For example, you will find ways to minimize, treat and clean up mould in the first chapter – Disaster Averted. Many questions pop up and I have tried to cover those asked the most often. As an example, all kinds of stains will be covered in the Laundry chapter, restoring burnt pans and reviving old cookware can be found in my Kitchen Rescue section, and what about the cleaning of the unmentionable toilet seat – that is covered too in Home Hacks. I then move into what I have described as my Clever Kitchen chapter, which provides around 25 recipes, tips and thrifty uses for food which may otherwise have been thrown away. The microwave has its own collection of quick low energy ideas followed by a number of recipes which have a 'flexi' option and can be cooked using whichever appliance you have available to you or seems the most appropriate to use that day. Last and by no means least, I decided to complete this book with a number of home-made gift ideas. This I think is a lovely warm, cosy, crafty type of chapter. I think there could be a gift idea for everyone in here and – just like everything else in this book – it is not going to cost the earth!

I will do my very best to share a sensible approach to living within budget, making do, mending and offering some real cost savings. If you're interested when I tell you I haven't bought a bottle of detergent for three years, I now oven-bake potatoes twenty at a time rather than two, have made the freezer and microwave my new best friends and am enjoying every green penny saving minute – then read on. Enough of the chit-chat, let's get down to it and save some money in a green-friendly way.

ENERGY

Does a day go by when we are not reminded about the rising cost of energy? Many of us have gone ahead to make simple changes that can help, including turning down thermostats, not heating empty rooms, boiling only the water we need when filling the kettle. Spend a few minutes getting to know your appliances so that you can become smart and savvy, understanding which ones are the energy guzzlers – probably something we didn't take into consideration before. I now give a second thought to whether the central heating goes on to heat every room in the house, and instead I confine the heating to one or two rooms, or the rooms most 'lived in'; the washing machine is used to wash a full load and not just one pair of jeans and I don't own a tumble dryer – they are first-class energy eaters.

I am beginning to enjoy prudence with energy use as I realize so much can be achieved from the one power source. For example, the oven may go on just once or twice a week, but when it does the heat is maximized and there may be a batch of meals cooked which can then be chilled, frozen and reheated later in the microwave. While I don't profess to be an energy expert, when it comes to the electricity consumed by various appliances, a good rule of thumb is that anything that is switched on to generate heat, i.e. ovens, tumble dryers, water heaters, electric radiators, blow heaters and kettles, will consume more electricity than those appliances that don't.

Fridges, freezers, washing machines (cold washing), low-energy lighting, microwave ovens and slow cookers are not huge energy eaters, so I would never listen to advice (that I have heard) that tells you to switch off fridges and freezers at night, for example – it's simply not worth the effort or risk. For me, this would be loaded with problems anyway, especially if I forgot to turn on the freezer the next morning! The best energy saving advice for fridges and freezers is to not leave the door open for longer than is necessary.

There is a lot of information out there that will explain exactly how much energy your own appliances use, and even the appliance's own handbook will supply a wealth of information. I have done some homework on mine and was surprised to learn the following:

- If using anything more than one large burner on my hob, it is cheaper to use my oven.
- A cold 20-degree long eco cycle in the washing machine of 2 hours uses a third of the energy of a 40-degree eco cycle.
- My microwave oven costs less than 1p per minute to run, so it is my 'go to' for a number of recipes included in this book.

While on the subject of what I call 'gadgets', there are so many to choose from. They are hitting the market at an alarming rate, promising to save energy costs and time, have their own recipe books and promise amazing results. My mind gets confused when I consider cooking that stretches beyond an oven, hob, microwave or pressure cooker. I am sure many of these appliances do a great job – some not so great – and even if the expense doesn't put me off, often finding a space to keep it becomes prohibitive.

My mind is taken back to when I bought an ice cream maker – at a fairly significant cost, I might add. I had seen them advertised and my friend had bought one too. I was desperate for one – what a great thing; I can make ice cream all of the

time. The grandchildren will love it and we can pick and choose our flavours! I bought boxes of cones, sprinkles and sauces – this was great! After an initial flurry of activity, needless to say, it is now gathering dust on the pantry floor. So, before I buy anything nowadays, the question I ask myself is, 'is this a need or a *want*?'

My gas central heating system is old, inefficient and very costly to run, so from a 'green living' point of view it is ridiculous. Apart from the running costs, its energy usage is probably obscene. I live in an old property that doesn't enjoy the benefits of double glazing and modern insulation, so when this ancient piece of kit is brought to life any warmth that is generated quickly escapes through the draughty windows and doors. It can be very cold inside my home on even the not-so-cold days, but nowadays I wrap up warm rather than turn on the heating. I am always on the move anyway, but when I do want to settle down in the rooms most used, the kitchen and the lounge are comfy and cosy.

The central heating is not used for now, but it is at the top of the list on my house refurbishment plan. What do I use for heat, you may ask? I have a wood-burning stove in the lounge and an Aga in the kitchen. For the critics out there who may suggest that neither of those appliances are eco-friendly, my response has to be – this is where I am right now. Twenty-five years ago, when I moved into my dream home and decided to invest in an Aga for cooking and a wood burner for heating, there were not the same pressures about energy consumption. I cannot afford to replace them at the moment, so instead I try to use them both sensibly and efficiently. A stove kettle sits on the wood burner so that when it is lit I am able to save on boiling an electric kettle. A potato wrapped in foil and placed on top of my wood burner will be baked a treat in an hour or so, only having to be turned once or twice and with no need to put the oven on.

Similarly, the heat generated by my Aga does the cooking, dries the laundry on a ceiling rack above it (when it can't be dried outside for free), heats my water for washing up, heats the room and will give any dry laundry folded neatly on the simmer plate a just-ironed look too. I hope that all readers after seeing some of the simple ideas I have used will examine their own ways of working and discover little energy saving tips of their own.

I think the point I am wanting to make is that all of our homes and our circumstances are quite different and many of our ways of living will not be considered the most eco-friendly.

Of course, I would love an energy efficient home with a ground-source heat pump, providing an ambient temperature in every room for minimal cost. I would have constant hot water, regular air changes, air conditioning in the summer months and every latest labour and energy saving gadget. However, I don't have any of the above; my house is draughty and cold, my heating system is probably obsolete, but I love my home and I have learned to make conscious decisions every day with my energy consumption, improved recycling, more reducing, less purchasing and therefore greener lifestyle choices.

MY MUCH-LOVED TOOL KIT

The following few recipes have been well documented in previous books, but as they are referred to in other recipes here – and will go on to be championed in the future, I am sure – I thought them worthy of being repeated. They all have so many uses, will save money in several areas and are simply now part of my everyday living toolkit, and I continue to find new uses for each of them.

Pure Magic

Pure Magic does exactly what it says – it is eco-friendly, very little is needed (just a squirt here or there) and it has so many uses. It really is magic!

You will need

500ml (17fl oz) heatproof measuring jug
spray bottle

200g (7oz) citric acid
150ml (5fl oz) just-boiled water
20ml (¾fl oz) eco-friendly washing-up liquid
10 drops essential oil (optional)

Place the citric acid in the heatproof measuring jug, pour over the just-boiled water and stir until completely dissolved – clear with no crystals remaining. Once cool, add the washing-up liquid and, if using, the essential oil for perfume. Leave the liquid in the jug to cool completely, uncovered, for a few hours, then transfer to a spray bottle.

USES: Tackles laundry stains (curry, fruit, tomato, grass, wine), is a natural whitener, dissolves limescale, green algae, kills mould, clears soap scum and is the best toilet cleaner.

While Pure Magic is a beast of a cleaner, it is not suitable for use on surfaces such as tables or worktops, because if it is not rinsed well it will dry sticky. It is an acidic cleaner, so it is not advised for use on natural stone, slate, granite or marble.

All-purpose Spray Cleaner

My daily cleaner all around the home – I absolutely love it. This solution has many uses, and it cuts through grease, dries to a shine and leaves no sticky residue.

You will need

300ml (10fl oz) spray bottle

60ml (2fl oz) white vinegar
150ml (5fl oz) water
40ml (1¼fl oz) surgical spirit (rubbing alcohol)
10–20 drops essential oil (optional)

Simply pour everything into the bottle, shake to combine, and it is good to go.

TIP: Try infusing your vinegar with leftover lemon or orange peels. In 2–3 days a large jar of white vinegar packed with used citrus will give the cleaning spray a gorgeous aroma and pale colour.

|||||||||||||||||||||||||||||||||||||||||||||||||||||||||||||||||||||||||||||||||||||||||||||||||||||||||||||||||||||||||||

USES: Everyday spray that's good for bathrooms, toilets, sinks, mirrors, glass, work surfaces, shower screens, sunglasses and car interiors. Spray directly onto a dry cleaning cloth then wipe it over computer and TV screens for an anti-static, streak-free shine and finish.

Since using this all-purpose spray on surfaces around the home it is no coincidence that insects refuse to pop by, as they hate the smell! Followers tell me the same too. House flies stay away and a number of followers struggling to deter ants have sprayed their floors and pantry shelves, only to find the ants made a quick exit.

I even found it to be an excellent insect repellent on my legs and arms when out gardening during the summer months. This isn't to say I would spray myself everyday with it as I am always a bit cautious about things that go on the skin – but it has saved my skin in a pinch. If you fancy giving it a go, as with anything new, do a patch test first.

Cream Cleaner

For those with granite and natural stone surfaces, where acidic cleaners are not advised, this cream cleaner, being gentle, non-abrasive and non-acidic, can be used safely. I even use it to remove scuff marks from my car.

You will need

400ml (14fl oz) glass jar with screw top
spoon

200g (7oz) bicarbonate of soda
70ml (2¼fl oz) vegetable glycerine
30ml (1fl oz) eco-friendly washing-up liquid (non-citrus
    scented)
a few drops of essential oil (optional)

Simply mix everything together in the jar using a spoon.

USES: Non-acidic cleaner that can be used widely for composite sinks, baths, stains on clothing, or as a hand cleaner, grout cleaner, shoe cleaner and silver cleaner.

General Polish

As well as for polishing furniture, I like to use this to treat wooden items that have maybe had to be washed and even (green) bleached because they were in a poor state due to dirt and, at worst, mould. This polish has also turned out to be a fantastic cleaner, degreaser and polish for stainless steel (especially cooker hoods), not to mention a quick spray-and-go shoe shine. A few sprays onto a dry duster then a rub over other leather items – such as handbags, cases and furniture – will add a rich lustre while softening the leather without leaving a greasy feel.

You will need

spray bottle
50ml (1¾fl oz) sunflower, vegetable or baby oil, the thinnest
and cheapest variety you have
30ml (1fl oz) white vinegar
30 drops essential oil (I like to use lavender)

Simply measure the ingredients into the bottle, shake, and it's
ready to go.

Lining Paste

This paste is a baker's dream, it keeps for weeks in the fridge
and is far cheaper than cake release sprays. This recipe makes
300g (10oz). Use gluten free flour or vegan shortening for
gluten free or vegan options.

You will need

large mixing bowl
hand-held electric whisk
jar with lid
100g (3½oz) vegetable shortening

100g (3½oz) flour (can replace with gluten-free)
100ml (3½fl oz) oil (I prefer vegetable or sunflower oil)

In mixing bowl, whisk the vegetable shortening and flour until thick and smooth. With the mixer running on a slow speed, pour in the oil in a thin, steady stream until you have a smooth paste the consistency of double cream. Transfer to the jar, seal with the lid and keep in the fridge to use from chilled. When ready to bake, brush the paste over your tin with a pastry brush, then add your cake batter.

USES: Any recipe that calls for the cooking vessel to be greased or lined.

Green Bleach

Since discovering natural oxygen bleach (or, my name for it, green bleach – it's less of a mouthful than sodium percarbonate) some years ago I have to say it has made the switch to 'green' easy and successful, and you can be safe in the knowledge that it isn't nasty like chlorine. The small white granules get to work immediately once activated in water, and have a limited life of only a few hours before completely decomposing into water, oxygen and soda ash.

Green bleach is expensive compared to harmful chlorine bleach, but I have learned to use it sparingly and only when necessary. It is mostly available online in the UK, though I have seen it on supermarket shelves in Europe, and followers world-wide tell me it is becoming more widely available. Let us hope it will not be long before you can find it on the shelf and at a better price in the UK, replacing the bottles of chlorine bleach.

I gather some countries have already banned chlorine bleach

from supermarket shelves. The switch to eco-friendly bleaching has been, for me, a complete lifestyle change and with every new cleaning challenge I discover crafty ways to introduce this wonder product with amazing results. I receive messages daily from converts and I hope this little section below helps to answer some of your questions. Those items of laundry with troublesome fixed unknown stains are no longer destined for the bin. There's no replacing of expensive clothing – budget win!

Here are some FAQs to get you started right:

If I add green bleach to my whites laundry is it actually doing any good at low temperatures, as I understand it needs boiling water to activate?

Boiling water will activate green bleach immediately, though it also works at low temperatures and even in cold water. Occasionally, when my kitchen sink is very stained, I have been busy, am rushing or need a clean that doesn't give me any work to do, I simply rinse the sink with cold water and let the water drain away. I then sprinkle over a teaspoon of green bleach granules, scrub them around with a sink brush, leave and either go to bed or go out. When I next visit the sink, it is bright white. Green bleach is non-acidic and therefore safe to use on my composite sink.

Can I make a green bleach spray to use as a toilet cleaner?

Sodium percarbonate once activated will only remain effective for a few hours, after which it decomposes into oxygen, water and natural soda ash – that is why it is so gorgeous for our planet's health and well-being. Unlike harmful chlorine bleach that hangs around in our ecosystem for years, is harmful to aquatic life and especially harmful to pets and children, a green bleach spray can be made but it needs to be used at once before it decomposes. It therefore cannot be made up and left on the shelf. I prefer instead to use my Pure Magic for toilets – it will do a much better and cheaper job and will remain active for weeks and weeks, sitting in its spray bottle on the shelf.

Stain removal – can I use green bleach on colours?

Unlike chlorine bleach, green bleach is not brutal and will not splash onto colours and immediately fade the fabric or leave a stain. When in doubt, I use half measures and do a tepid soak as follows. In a washing-up bowl, dissolve 2–3 tablespoons of washing soda and ½ teaspoon of green bleach together in around one litre of just-boiled water, then add cold water to bring the solution temperature to tepid. Add the stained, coloured items and leave to soak overnight. The next day, remove the items and squeeze out the surplus solution, then pop them into the drum of the washing machine for a long, eco 20°C cycle.

How can I get my kids' white cotton polo tops and socks white again?

Save them up and maybe wash them once or twice a week along with a whites load. The night before, add a cup of washing soda and 2–3 teaspoons of green bleach to a bucket, then pour over boiling water to activate. Stir with a wooden spoon and top up with cold water so that the bucket is two-thirds full and the water is tepid in temperature. Add the socks and tops and soak overnight. The next day, wring them out, then transfer to the drum of the washing machine and wash at 20°C.

There are times, followers tell me, when the stains are still not all gone – not just children's clothes but adults' too. If the results are not bright white or a stubborn stain refuses to budge, then we need the 'hot water' treatment – but be cautious because very hot water may shrink fabrics; I tend to use this as a last resort. Pop the very soiled socks, tops or other stained items into a bucket or basin, add the washing soda and bleach as before, then add very hot water to fill to two-thirds full. Leave the items to soak overnight. I have used the hot water soak on colours too.

Can I fix scorches on fabrics?

We all know that an iron that's too hot will scorch, and as long as the scorch isn't too dark then a green bleach soak will blank it out successfully. I've scorched a white cotton pillow-case, and in the past even chlorine bleach would result in a pink hue to the scorch, yet green bleach will whiten that mark successfully. I popped the pillowcase into a bowl, sprinkled over 2 teaspoons of green bleach, poured over a kettle of just-boiled water and left it for a few hours.

I have seen oxygen bleach available in the supermarket – is this green bleach?

Many followers have excitedly messaged me to say they have discovered green bleach on local supermarket shelves, however make sure what you're buying is the real deal. Some brands offer a blend that's usually around 35 per cent green bleach (sodium percarbonate) and the rest is made up of washing soda (sodium carbonate). It is an effective whitener but it's not as versatile as having the two ingredients separately to be able to adjust the dose to fit different jobs. It can be expensive, too – penny for penny it costs more than buying the two products separately.

DISASTER AVERTED

n this chapter I hope to cover some of those 'panic' situations where instinct may be telling you to do one thing, but in fact the best way may be entirely different. When in a panic, stop, take a breather and have a think.

For example, water is not always the answer when it comes to cleaning up soot, brick dust and mud – nor do I dampen mould on a pair of shoes or boots. Then there are the times when water has caused the problems, creating a mark on your wooden table or pooling as condensation onto your window-sills and marking your curtains and furnishings. Rather than rushing out to buy what may be considered to be solutions to the disaster, or at worst thinking that the item needs to be discarded – let us first consider our options, apply our know-ledge and try to resolve the problem using the skills and ingredients that we already have.

FIXING MOULD

High energy prices, along with a conscience about consuming the Earth's limited resources, means many of us are drastically reducing our energy consumption both in and around the home. Central heating and portable heating appliances are way up there when it comes to eating away at the household budget, and during the winter months it makes much more sense to heat only the rooms in use, to turn the heating down and no longer heat unused areas.

I was once invited out for a magical afternoon tea at a large eighteenth-century country house owned by the National Trust. The house, its grounds and history had me transported back to a world of opulence, antique furniture and beautiful ball gowns. However, looking at the vastness of the rooms, the high decorated ceilings and sprawling single-glazed windows, no fitted carpets and certainly no central heating, I couldn't help but wonder how cold these houses must have been in wintertime. Each room boasted a decorative fireplace, but even so these rooms must have been absolutely freezing! I was then told that there were hangers for coats and capes outside each door so that residents could pop on an extra layer when walking from room to room!

Thankfully, my home is not so cold that I need to wear a coat around the house, but clearly the downside to reducing heating and ventilation in the home is that if there are any damp situations in the house they soon become a playground for mould, which if left unchecked is not only unsightly but can also be harmful to health.

Mould on Walls, Paintwork and Wallpaper

When considering how to tackle a growth of mould spores inside the home, it is worth thinking about why it is happening. For example, I had a mould patch behind a chest of drawers in a downstairs room, but as well as cleaning it up I needed to find its cause. The mould was forming on an outside-facing wall, and when I examined outside I could see that the down-pipe from the roof fed into a drain that had become blocked with leaves. So every time it rained, the drain overflowed and excess moisture soaked into the bricks, making its way through the internal plaster then growing mould spores on the wallpaper behind the furniture.

This isn't to suggest that all mould is due to some leaking gutter or pipe, but it's always worth checking for a source. If the problem persists regardless, the mould may be due to building flaws. For example, I have a persistent damp patch due to the fact that an outside path was laid many years past which breaches (is above) the damp-proof course of the house – it will be fixed one day, I hope, but in the meantime the mould has to be treated instead.

You will need

> 2 tbsp bicarbonate of soda
> warm, damp cloth

When I read that bicarbonate of soda has a pH of around 8 to 8.1, which is too high for mould to thrive, it was music to my ears! Bicarb, as we know, cleans and deodorizes, so here I considered I had a three-in-one natural cleaning solution for the mould on my walls. It would kill it, clean it and neutralize any damp odours. I know from experience that, just like soot (see page 38), wetting mould with water simply makes it more difficult to clean.

When the source had been detected (in my case, the drain) I started with cleaning up outside – ensuring the drain was clear and free-flowing again so that the mould wouldn't return. Inside, a warm, slightly dampened cloth dipped into dry bicarbonate of soda was enough to clean off the speckles of black, unsightly mould. My wall has a wallpaper covering, so again, I had to be sure I didn't overwet the area and damage the covering. A painted wall would withstand a tougher rub.

My persistent mould problem due to the breached damp-proof membrane gets the same treatment. I reach for my damp cloth dipped in dry bicarb to clean the inside wall – repeating as and when it recurs.

Home-made Moisture Absorber

Mould can grow anywhere and the cause is always the build-up of excess moisture that doesn't readily evaporate. Mould on window frames and around windows, on curtains and blinds is usually due to condensation forming on the windows when the warm, moist air in the room hits the cold glass and immediately condenses and forms water droplets.

The windows steam up as more water condenses, then the windows run with rivers of water, pooling onto the windowsill, soaking into the curtains or blinds. As the water doesn't dry immediately, mould spores begin to grow in corners, around the frames and on the fabrics, and next time you look there are unsightly black spots. Mould hates fresh air, so the best preventative measure is good ventilation – although I realize this is easier said than done when it may be snowing and blowing outside! Opening the bathroom window following a shower to allow steam to escape, or using an extractor fan when cooking is always a good habit and ensures moisture doesn't hang around. When this isn't possible, and for spots that tend to get a little damp, a simple home-made 'moisture absorber' can be added to problem areas – a windowsill is a good place for this.

You will need

small bowl or watertight box

50–100g bicarbonate of soda (but do experiment to see how long it takes for the bicarb to clump in your affected area)

Simply pour the bicarbonate of soda into the bowl or box and place in an out of the way position as close to the problem area as you can get it. The bicarbonate of soda will suck water vapour from the air and eventually turn lumpy as it dampens.

When spent and my bicarb powder has turned into damp lumps, I then use it as a water softener – 1–2 tablespoons in the dish washing-up water will give me more bubbles, meaning I can use less washing-up liquid.

I also have a jar of silica sachets (you know, the little packets that you'll get in new handbags, suitcases, etc.). Silica gel absorbs moisture, so I've found that putting a few sachets in a fancy dish is a good alternative to bicarbonate of soda boxes, but keep these away from children – those little sachets can look tempting to little hands.

Mould on Fabrics

Many followers have messaged me in a panic when they have seen that pools of condensation from windows have been absorbed by a curtain lining or fabric blind, but have only been discovered once the damp fabric, unable to quickly dry out, has developed a mould patch.

Washing often doesn't remove the mould, and it may be that the fabrics need to be dry-cleaned anyway, so I have two methods that I use. Cleaning large fabric areas may well be easier using method 2.

Method 1

You will need

    an old soft-bristled toothbrush
    warm soapy water and cloth

    Pure Magic spray (see page 12)

Apply a fine spray of Pure Magic to the mould spots and massage it in using the toothbrush. The Pure Magic will destroy any mould spores and help to remove the staining, however it can dry leaving a sticky or white residue, so it is important that after using you wipe the area with a sponge or cloth and warm soapy water to remove any residual Pure Magic. It is not necessary to overwet the area, a gentle wipe is sufficient.

If there are any speckles of mould remaining, Mother Nature may well come to the rescue . . . I recall a mould problem that

I created myself. I had a brand-new white t-shirt that I discovered I had stained, so that night I popped it into a bowl of cold water. The next day I wrung out the shirt, pleased to see the stain had disappeared, and transferred it to the washing machine, intending to add in a whites load. However, I never got around to it and forgot about the brand-new, wet t-shirt sitting in the washing machine drum until several days later. To my horror, there were tiny mould spots absolutely all over the white t-shirt. The mould had the perfect place to grow – damp, warm and no air circulating. Not to worry, I thought, I can run a whites wash right now and the mould will disappear. However, it did not – after the wash it was still well and truly there.

Purely coincidentally, the sun was shining that day – perfect for drying. So I hung out the mould-speckled white shirt in full sun along with the rest of the laundry. To my utter delight and disbelief, when it was dry, the mould spores were gone – every trace. Skipping back into the house, I celebrated the fact that Mother Nature had all the answers!

So, back to the curtains and blinds – even though there may be traces of mould that you can't remove, if you can expose them to full sunshine while still dampened by the Pure Magic treatment, any residue should bleach out. Even a bright sunny windowsill will do the job. It doesn't have to go outside.

Method 2

Let us say you have huge, heavy, thick, lined curtains or blinds, and upon examination as part of your spring clean you discover water stains and spots of mould on the fixed linings or bottom of the blinds. The thought of grappling with these heavy drapes to try to remove this mould fills you with dread.

If you can take down the curtains or blinds to treat them, that is much easier, especially if you can get them outside on a sunny day. However, this can also be done as an inside job – but it will take a little longer if the drapes are so large that they can't be taken down.

You will need

medium mixing bowl
measuring jug and spoons
wooden spoon
shower puff
2 old, clean, dry towels

2 tbsp washing soda
2 tsp green bleach (see page 17)
200ml (7fl oz) just-boiled water
2 tbsp eco-friendly washing-up liquid
100ml (3½fl oz) cold water

Add the washing soda and green bleach to the bowl, pour over the just-boiled water and stir until completely dissolved and beginning to foam. Then add the washing-up liquid and cold water. Using the shower puff, work at the solution until the bowl is filled with white suds.

Lay the mould-affected areas of the curtain linings (usually the hems) over an old towel on a table or take the table to the window if the curtains haven't been taken down. Position the towel between the curtain and the lining to protect the main fabric and treat only the linings. If the linings are fixed at the hem, then I would still attempt the clean, but taking extra special care not to overwet the curtains by regularly wiping down the treated area with the dry towel. Rub the shower puff packed with green bleach suds over a workable section, massaging well into the affected areas. Do not overwet the fabric, and as each area is treated wipe it over with the other clean, dry towel.

Leave to dry in a warm, airy room, and if there is a sunny windowsill to offer them up to, even better. The mould spots and winter grime will be cleaned away.

Mould on Wood

I have a treasured wooden step stool that the grandchildren, when they were little tots, used to stand on so that they could reach my level to help me bake. The children got big and the stool for some reason ended up being used outside and in the garage and became well and truly neglected. I discovered it one summer's day and was saddened to see it filthy, splashed with paint and mouldy in parts – with that black, penetrating mould that is difficult to remove.

However, I managed to get it clean in the end, with this cleaning method. This uses green bleach. A word of warning when using green bleach on wood – do make sure it is fully dissolved in the water, otherwise it will leave a bleached white patch on the wood.

You will need

> small brush
> round-bladed knife (to remove the paint)
> clean cloths

hot soapy water
cream cleaner (see page 14)
1 tsp green bleach (see page 17) fully dissolved in 100ml
   (3½fl oz) just-boiled water
home-made general polish (see page 15)

Start by cleaning the wood with hot soapy water, a small brush
and some cream cleaner. When working away at my beloved
step stool I found I was easily able to scrape off the paint
splashes because the cream cleaner had actually loosened the
paint.

While the wood is still wet, either paint or spray the dissolved
green bleach onto the wood, paying particular attention to the
mouldy areas. Leave the bleach to soak for an hour, then rinse
off well with a cloth and warm soapy water, then leave to dry.

Once dry, finish off with a spray and a wipe of home-made
general polish. I found this brought the step stool back to its
former glory, and now it is back in the kitchen.

Mould on Leather Goods: Bags and Shoes

Mould loves dark, damp, stuffy and cool conditions. If you
keep shoes, boots and leather goods in the bottom of a non-
ventilated wardrobe, cupboard or shoe store and one item is
put away not quite dry, you may discover when you go to pick
up your favourite shoes sometime later that the bag or leather
item has grown a layer of grey mould. The smell can be pretty
awful too.

A picture from a follower springs to mind. They had a pair
of dark blue suede evening shoes and a leather and canvas
handbag that had been in a loft, and both were so completely

taken over by the fusty-smelling furry grey fungus that they were hardly recognizable.

This method will clean off that unsightly mould, and if you infuse the bicarbonate of soda with lavender, the smell will be neutralized straight away, too.

You will need

old dry towel or piece of paper
warm, light, airy room
soft clothes brush

sugar shaker filled with bicarbonate of soda
dried lavender buds (added to the shaker for perfume –
optional)

First, dust the item all over with bicarbonate of soda – put plenty on, sprinkling on the outside and inside of the item. Using a sugar shaker makes the bicarb go further and enables you to get an even sprinkle into every nook and cranny. Stand the item on an old dry towel or piece of paper and leave in a warm, light, airy room. Mould spores thrive in damp, dank conditions, so presenting them with dry warm air and bicarb will soon finish them off.

After a day or so, take the item outside and gently shake off the surplus powder, then finish off with a soft brush to remove any residual powder plus the dried-out furry mould.

Permanent Mould Stains

I realize this may not be a fix for every mould-stained item, especially if it is very large, not washable or dark-coloured, but I used this really successfully on a very mouldy strap from a child's trike. The trike had been stored over the winter in a shed, and once brought out the white strap harness (similar to the strap of a rucksack) was not just dotted with black mould – it was covered. I washed it, but the mould stains remained and made the straps look dirty and unsightly. The following worked brilliantly – the first part of the method involves a little work, then the second stage and the finishing touches are performed by Mother Nature herself – in saving a much-loved toy.

You will need

medium mixing bowl
sunny day

2 tbsp washing soda
1 tsp green bleach (see page 17)
600–700ml (20–24fl oz) just-boiled water
Pure Magic spray (see page 12)

First, place the item in the bowl and sprinkle over the washing soda and green bleach powders, then pour over sufficient just-boiled water to cover. The solution will froth, but there will be no nasty smells. Leave the item to soak overnight, then have a good look the next day – the mould may well have disappeared, which is great, but if there is still any residual staining, move on to the next step.

Peg the item on the washing line in full sun while still wet, give it a quick squirt with Pure Magic spray and leave it there for a day or maybe longer, until the cleaning and whitening is complete. Leave the item outside come rain or shine – I promise Mother Nature and Pure Magic will complete the task, though she cannot be rushed.

Once completely dried and stain-free, bring the item back inside. Pure Magic can cause fabrics to dry stiffly but a clean rinse and dry and it will be fine – it really depends how much you used.

STINKY SPILLS – DON'T CRY OVER SPILT MILK!

. . . Even though it can leave a lingering smell and stain – especially in the car! I remember years ago – frazzled, tired, hungry – I was busily fitting in a supermarket shop after work one winter evening. I came home, loaded myself up with too many bags to comfortably carry from the car, and then went on to drop one on the ground. Furious when I saw items strewn across the drive, I let go of the other bag and dropped it back into the boot of the car so that I had two hands free to pick everything up. Having picked up all the items on the ground and popped them back into the bag, I then returned to the boot of the car and the rest of the shopping. Can you believe! The bag I had dropped back into the car in my panic had managed to break open a container of milk. It was everywhere. Splattered over the rest of my food shopping and, worst of all, over the carpet in the boot. Why is it that when things spill, there seems to be more than the volume that was in the container? These things always happen at the worst time. I wanted to shut the car door, leave the shopping and cry!

To cut a long story short, the smell never did leave the car, but if I knew then what I know now, the memory of that day would have long since passed. This is my go-to recipe for all of those spills or accidents, which if not dealt with at the outset can leave a long-lasting residual odour or stain. I'm thinking milk, red wine, vomit, diarrhoea, urine, juice – those very difficult pet and baby accidents.

You will need

absorbent paper
rubber gloves (optional depending on stain)
medium bowl
clean dry cloth
old dry towel

600ml (20fl oz) tepid water
6 tbsp white vinegar
2–3 drops eco-friendly washing-up liquid

There is usually a certain amount of panic associated with a spill or stain of this kind, and instinctively you may want to rush for a bowl of hot water. My advice is to take a breather and weigh up the situation. A large spill or accident will need to be mopped up first, so absorbent paper is quick and does the job, soaking up surplus milk, wine, vomit, etc. You may want to pop on the gloves too!

Don't rub at any of the spill; continue to dab at it with paper until most of the moisture has been lifted and only a malodorous stain remains. You will note that the recipe here calls for tepid water, and this is essential as hot water is not good for carpets, plus it can fix a stain and an odour.

So, once you've mopped up, add the tepid water to the bowl, then the vinegar and finally the washing-up liquid. Creating a froth with the washing-up liquid is not necessary, and I prefer a simple clear solution so I can better see what's happening to the stain.

Starting at the outside edge of the stain, dab (don't rub) it with a cloth that has been dampened with the water solution.

The tepid water will help release the stain, the vinegar will clean and neutralize and the washing-up liquid will dissolve any fat in the spilt milk, etc. Refrain from overwetting the carpet and, most of all, take your time. Rinse the cloth regularly and you will see that the stain has dissolved into it.

Finally, dab the area with a dry towel and leave to air-dry naturally. I remember posting this on social media one time to then receive a message from a specialist carpet cleaner who confirmed that this is very similar to the treatment they use on hand-woven carpets. That made my day!

DRY CLEAN-UP OF SOOT, BRICK DUST AND MUD

Soot from candles, fires, matches and even fingers can leave its dreadful mark anywhere – on carpets, wallpaper, soft furnishings and clothing. Instinctively we want to rub and scrub it away, but then we find the black smudging looks ten times worse. I find the best treatment is to 'dry clean' – with no water in sight.

You will need

clean dry cloth
vacuum cleaner
soft dry sponge

sugar shaker filled with bicarbonate of soda

Soot, brick dust and mud would love you to wet it, so it can spread itself far and wide. Instead, sprinkle dry bicarbonate of soda over the soot stain then brush or rub it in gently with your fingers. Keep going until there is no trace of soot – more than one application may be necessary. Use a dry cloth to move the bicarb into the carpet pile or fabric, then use a vacuum cleaner to remove all traces of both soot and bicarbonate of soda.

If the soot mark is on a wall – say from a candle – dip a cloth very slightly dampened with warm water into a saucer of bicarb and gently dab at the soot staining. Once the bicarb has adhered to the sooty wall, use a soft dry sponge to work at the stain until it leaves the wall without a trace.

This 'dry' treatment is also my go-to for muddy paw prints – you know the ones. Picture a cream carpet and the perfect imprint of a paw . . . Instinctively there is the panic; the dog is chastised even though he has no idea that his wet feet are any different to his dry feet of yesterday; and the carpet is unsightly, so maybe you reach for a bowl of water to clean it. Try instead to take a deep breath – calm down, stroke the dog and apologize, then just leave the paw print (or shoe print) to dry out completely – it may take a day. Once dried, sprinkle over the dry bicarbonate of soda, gently work it into the carpet pile, then vacuum up.

BROKEN GLASS

I remember a time when I got the tiniest piece of glass in my foot, and oh my goodness, the pain! I couldn't see it but I could certainly feel it. We have all squealed with terror when a full drink or any glass is accidentally broken on a hard floor. The shards go everywhere and there is immediate panic as children, dogs and cats are banished from the room. Hopefully no one has been hurt and the glass tumbler can be replaced. The responsible adult takes charge and collects all of the large visible pieces, and even though it may look as if every piece has been fished from the pool of spilt drink, tiny shards will often still remain. The floor then has to be cleaned. The spilt milk, juice, wine or whatever was in the glass vessel requires cleaning, of course, but then there is the fear that unseen tiny shards of glass will wriggle their way into a mop or cloth – to make a spiky reappearance when least expected, maybe causing injury.

You will need

bread
mop and bucket

Before reaching for the mop and bucket to clean up the spills, or for sheets of dry kitchen paper, I instead arm myself with a few slices of bread – giving me a handy 5cm (2in) or so thickness. Using my thick 'bread sponge' I mop up the spills while at the same time gathering up any minuscule shards of glass. This single-use sponge I then pop into a used flour or sugar bag and into the bin.

Compared to kitchen paper, bread does a much better job. Dry kitchen paper may well mop up the spilt drink but I have discovered it can leave those tiny glass shards behind. Bread, on the other hand, not only soaks up the spills but gathers the glass too. Then I can safely mop the floor and allow the dogs and kids back into the room.

CRAZED PORCELAIN

I have a couple of oval plates, both identical, yet one became stained and marked. I can best describe it as 'crazed', and this happened after I stupidly put it into a hot oven. I remember being so disappointed, but I only had myself to blame. The beautiful plate ended up separated from its partner, to be hidden away at the back of the cupboard, destined to eventually be cast aside because it looked both dirty and damaged. A very hot dishwasher cycle can do this too, but I know in my case both me and the oven were the culprits. As I became more and more adventurous with green bleach (see page 17), I did wonder whether it could work its magic on this plate – and you've probably guessed, of course it did!

You will need

bowl large enough to hold the plate or item

2 tsp green bleach
just-boiled water to cover

Lay the damaged crazed item in a roomy bowl, measure over the bleach, then pour over the water and leave to soak for 2–3 hours. Green bleach only remains active for a few hours, so an overnight soak is not necessary. Remove from water, wipe dry and it should be good as new.

LEAKY RADIATOR RUST ON CARPETS

I have included this little tip because a rust mark or stain from a leaking radiator can be both unsightly and a very annoying discovery, especially when the carpet is fairly new. Proprietary carpet shampoo is unlikely to improve the situation; in fact it can make things even worse. I have used this treatment on two occasions – once on a brand new cream carpet and secondly on a bedroom carpet where the leak from the radiator was so severe that a blackened rust mark appeared not only underneath the radiator but was so bad that it actually stained the floor under a metal castor of a nearby piece of furniture.

You will need

cotton pad
small bowl of warm water
old dry towel

Pure Magic spray (see page 12)
table salt (optional)

Before diving in with the treatment, I always recommend a test area first to make sure the carpet dye isn't affected. A little spray then a quick dab with a cotton pad on the affected area should result in the stain lifting almost immediately. Once happy that the carpet colour is not affected, you can spray the rust spot around the radiator and, in my case, into the carpet dent that had also attracted a rust stain.

Leave for a few minutes then use the cotton pad to work at the rust and water damage – dabbing, not rubbing. The stain should dissolve readily, but if the rust stain is old or the marks are particularly stubborn, then try adding a sprinkle of table salt too and leave a little longer.

Once the stain has resolved then it is important that any Pure Magic is removed from the carpet because otherwise it will dry sticky. Rinse out the cotton pad in the bowl of warm water and dab at the carpet repeatedly, rinsing regularly until the stain and any traces of Pure Magic and salt have been removed. Do not overwet the carpet.

Once all is clean, dab dry with the old clean towel.

LAUNDRY

Those who know me well or have my previous books will remember I have been known to (effectively I might add – and it's a lot of fun!) use ivy leaves and conkers to provide me with 'freebie' laundry detergent. Mother Nature's wonders such as these have been a huge 'going green' thrill for me. I understand, though, that this is potentially quite labour-intensive, and needing to get out and forage before putting the washer on is not going to be practical for everyone. I certainly remember the days when the washer seemed to be on constantly, there was work to go to, the kids to get off to school, the supermarket shop, meals to plan, cleaning to do, and certainly nipping out with a basket to cut ivy leaves before washing the school shirts was never going to happen! Here is a collection of my favourite go-to tips for almost any laundry issue. I like to boast that I have not bought a bottle of laundry detergent in years – I must be saving a fortune! Instead of spending money, I spend a little time once a month making bulk supplies of liquid soap that does a sterling job in both the washing machine and on hand-washed delicates. I mix a quick box of powder detergent too and save small bottles to store handy quantities of travel wash. Drying laundry in the fresh outdoors and letting the sun 'kiss' clean even the most difficult stains will leave you feeling quite smug as you realize that the natural way is not only the cheapest; it is the best.

TO STEAM OR NOT TO STEAM?

Growing up, I don't remember the steam iron until my grandmother got one, when I think I was about twelve years old. I have vague recollections before that of an electric flat iron and a dampened sheet of muslin cloth being used over very stubborn creases.

Nowadays the steam iron is commonplace; it is effective in quickly smoothing out wrinkles and creases and is probably a must in every household. I know there are those people who say they gave up ironing years ago and as long as clothes are well folded when they come out of the tumble dryer then ironing isn't necessary. I have not had a tumble dryer for nearly fifty years. I remember buying one and running it for a few months until I got the electricity bill, then saw how expensive it was to run. I quickly sold it on and have not been tempted to have once since.

Laundry in my house is air-dried for free, either hung outside to blow in the fresh air or hung on a ceiling clothes rack indoors when the weather doesn't work for outside drying. Maybe I am old-fashioned but I do like crease-free clothes and laundry – or, should I say, I like the creases in the right place. Of course, for those dressmakers amongst us the iron is an essential tool if a finished piece of work is to be gorgeous.

If you have ever thought about the electricity consumed by the iron and wondered whether it can be reduced, I believe it can and I am enjoying my new approach.

My go-to used to be to fill my iron with water then switch it on and wait for it to reach its high temperature, when the water inside would be hot enough to make steam. I would then set to work on my pile of ironing. If I was impatient and tried to start too soon and the water was not quite up to temperature, the iron would leak and leave water marks on my clothes. Sometimes this created a stain.

Similarly, if my iron was too hot, even on a steam setting, and I touched it even ever so lightly onto my best silk blouse, polyester top or fine wool jumper, then I could find myself with the best part of the sleeve stuck to the iron, resulting in my blouse, top or jumper being ruined for ever and a black sticky mess on the iron plate to remind me of the crisis.

I found that when using a steam iron, leaving water in the iron between uses causes extra limescale build-up and the water can go green inside. The benefits of using a dry iron – apart from the obvious energy savings – are that there is no limescale damage to the iron and less water is consumed overall, and the life of your appliance is also extended. If you do continue to favour steam for ironing, empty the water tank between uses and leave the flap open to allow air to circulate.

I decided to think about how I could move forward in an energy efficient, green way when doing the ironing – one of those household tasks that, maybe weirdly, I find quite relaxing. I have to say that since using this method I realize there is no fear of scorching, melting of fabrics or limescale wear and tear on my iron. I am enjoying a saving of both energy and money.

I decided to switch from steam to 'dry', with a separate spray water bottle on the side to help with stubborn creases when fabrics are too dry.

When it comes to my ironing, the clothes are first sorted into piles. Pile one is for nylons, polyester, silks, synthetics and woollens. Pile two is for cottons, and pile three is for working clothes. I turn my iron onto its lowest (synthetics) setting and start to work on pile number one along with my spray bottle of water if the clothes are really dry and the creases need a helping hand. No scorching, no snagging or melting – the iron can never get too hot.

When ready to move onto pile two, the dry iron temperature is now increased to medium, which on my iron states woollens. This temperature setting is still less than the steam setting and I am very pleased to announce is as high as I need to go – even with cottons.

My water mist is applied, ironing is completed and then I turn the iron off. Pile three – any working clothes – is ironed for free using the residual heat from the iron with no fear of water splashes or stains from the cooling water inside the iron.

I cannot tell you how happy 'dry ironing' has made me and I wonder why I haven't done it sooner. Less energy, less water, less wear and tear on my iron, and I feel as though I have made an amazing discovery – only to realize this is how it was done for centuries!

If clothes have been air-dried outside or inside and they are brought in or taken down (folded, by the way, not slung in a heap into the basket) just before they are 'bone dry', as my grandmother would say, then they are perfect for ironing and no spray or steam is even necessary.

LIQUID DETERGENT

When it comes to detergent, a quick glance at the reverse label will confirm our fears that biological detergents in particular are harmful to the environment. There are eco-friendly alternatives to choose from, but the prices can be four times those of supermarket own-branded chemical-heavy equivalents.

This recipe will save you a fortune, and for busy households I feel it is a winner – we make this in bulk, around 4 litres (8.5 pints) in one go!

You will need

large knife
chopping board
digital weighing scales
hand blender with bowl attachment, or use a grater or
   potato masher
your largest saucepan or bowl
measuring jug
spatula or wooden spoon
5 x 1-litre (34fl oz) plastic bottles (I use orange juice bottles
   – labels removed, washed and labelled with permanent
   marker)
funnel

150g (5½oz) soap slivers and/or single use hotel soaps
1 litre (34fl oz) just-boiled water
150g (5½oz) washing soda crystals

20ml (¾fl oz) eco-friendly washing-up liquid
up to 2.6 litres (5.5 pints) cold water
few drops of food or soap colour (optional)
few drops of lavender essential oil for fragrance (or fragrance
     of choice, optional)

Once I have collected enough soap slivers I make a batch of detergent. Alternatively, use a bar of your favourite soap. Using the knife and board cut the soap into small slices to make it easier to blitz. Transfer to the blender and blitz to a fine powder. If you don't have a blender the soap can be grated into small pieces, the finer the better. Transfer the soap powder to the large saucepan and pour over the just-boiled water. Stir with the spatula or wooden spoon until the soap has completely dissolved and no lumps remain.

Add the washing soda and stir through – if it clumps, use the hand blender to blitz it, and if you don't have a stick blender then a potato masher will do the job. Once completely smooth, add the washing-up liquid and 1 litre (34fl oz) of the cold water and stir well. The detergent will thicken substantially as it cools, so as it does, add a further 1 litre (34fl oz) of cold water, stir well, then leave to go completely cold.

Once cold, if the detergent remains thick and gloopy add the remaining 600ml (20fl oz) cold water along with a few drops of food or soap colour and lavender essential oil (or fragrance of choice), if you like.

Once you have a thick creamy consistency you're happy with, pour the mixture into the bottles using the funnel. Fill the bottles, leaving a gap of around 7.5cm (3in) at the top, because often the detergent thickens further while sitting. If this happens, add a little more water, give it a shake and the consistency is fine.

Commercial detergents add surfactants, which prevent thickening and separation of the contents. When I tried to do some reading and research on surfactants my head turned to scrambled egg – it's an absolute minefield of chemicals (some okay-sounding, some not), so I am happy that my detergent may thicken a little in the bottle.

You may be wondering – why not add all of the water at the start of the detergent making? I have found that not all soaps need the same amount of water, so it is better to add it in stages. I made one batch using a bar of pure soap that hardly thickened at all, so I added about 20g (¾oz) of grated everyday soap and it thickened up perfectly.

To use

I add 2–3 tablespoons of washing soda into the detergent drawer for every wash as I live in a very hard-water area. I use 100ml (3½fl oz) of the detergent in a small plastic cup and place it straight into the drum and in with the laundry. I have used it for the heaviest-soiled items, always on a long, eco, 20°C cold wash, with perfect results. I use it too for hand-washing of woollens and delicate fabrics – 80ml (2½fl oz) for a hand wash.

TRAVEL WASH

Holiday time is fun but it can also be stressful, especially when travelling with kids or pets.

The supermarkets offer us a range of products in handy small travel packs to add to our stocks of sunscreen, shampoo, conditioners, etc. Amongst the supply are the small, expensive, single-use plastic bottles of detergent. Here is a handy little recipe (adapted from the detergent recipe) – the dried ingredients can be added to a reusable plastic bottle to be reconstituted once at your destination. There's no fear of a bottle exploding all over your clothes in the suitcase, no liquids to declare, no extra weight to carry and no unnecessary expense.

You will need

digital weighing scales
hand blender with bowl attachment, coffee grinder or hand
  grater
funnel
500ml (17fl oz) plastic bottle

15g (½oz) soap slivers
20g (¾oz) washing soda
2–3 drops eco-friendly washing-up liquid

Add the soap slivers to the blender bowl, or use a coffee grinder or grater to break the soap into a fine powder or the smallest pieces possible. Pop the funnel into the neck of the bottle and transfer the soap powder followed by the measured washing soda, then add 2–3 drops of the washing-up liquid. Screw on the cap then pack into the suitcase.

Once on holiday, fill the bottle with hand-hot water, give it a shake and the detergent is ready to use. Use to soak swimwear – it'll dissolve sun cream and oil and it's great for hand-washing any garment while on holiday.

This bottle of travel detergent was my saviour while travelling with Wilfred the dog when he was a puppy. He had not been on a long car journey before – just short trips here and there – and what he had facing him was a journey of several hours. We stopped regularly to exercise him, though he seemed baffled by this ever-so-long trip. We were motoring along nicely, the sun shining, looking forward to having some time away. Music on in the car, enjoying the views, when this distinct odour from the rear of the car found its way to the front. Shock, horror, stress and panic when I realized Wilfred had messed. We pulled off the road and found a quiet, car-free country lane to examine the situation. The dog seat cover, which is a large, custom-fitted, quilted suede-type fabric had not just dog mess – it was a diarrhoea mess! I had kitchen paper, thankfully, to clean up most of it, but I was left with staining and an obvious odour. I then remembered my travel wash. I activated my detergent with cold drinking water, gave it a shake, massaged it into the accident, then wiped it as clean and dry as I could before putting the cover back into the car. I have to say there was no smell whatsoever (washing soda is very good with odours) and once we reached our destination the dog car cover was simply soaked overnight in a tepid washing-soda solution in the bath then hung out to air-dry (it is too big for the washing machine). Needless to say, I don't go on any trips with Wilfred now without my travel wash!

POWDER DETERGENT

This powder detergent recipe is an alternative to the liquid option and can be quickly mixed in a jar or plastic container. I find it is better suited to a long 20°C eco cycle, rather than a short thirty-minute cycle for example. Powder takes longer to dissolve than liquid detergent and may not fully dissolve during a short low-temperature cycle. For short cycles or hand-washing I use the liquid detergent.

I like this detergent because it can be adjusted to suit your own water type. If you live in a hard water area then add more washing soda, which will further soften the water. If you want a detergent that you will use just for 'whites' then add a teaspoon of green bleach to the detergent drawer at the same time as the powder detergent mix.

I have included washing soda because of its natural water softening, anti-bac and stain removal properties, bicarbonate of soda to soften the water and prevent the build-up of lime-scale and Epsom salts to remove odours. I have found that the laundry smells fresh and feels soft and lovely after using this detergent, especially when a favourite essential oil is added.

You will need

large jar or plastic tub with a lid
digital weighing scales
tbsp scoop or measure
spoon to stir

5 drops essential oil of choice for perfume (optional; I try to
   avoid citrus because it can cause the detergent to clump)
A drizzle of eco-friendly washing-up liquid (½tsp) – I find it
   helps to prevent lumps

200g (for soft water) or 300g (for hard water) washing
   soda
250g bicarbonate of soda
100g Epsom salts

Weigh all of the ingredients into the large jar or tub then stir
well using the spoon. Add the essential oil and washing-up
liquid, screw on the lid then give the whole lot a really good
shake. I use 3 tablespoons per load into the detergent drawer
– adding in 1-2 teaspoons green bleach for a brighter, whiter
wash.

GET SAVVY WITH STAINS

How many items of clothing have you tossed out because of a stain? Biological detergents and stain-removing products are expensive and – if my followers are anything to go by – they very often don't work. Many people make contact after they have exhausted every avenue, every product they can find, to no avail. So many of the questions and queries I receive are about stains, and there are always outliers and those that are remarkably stubborn – you have no idea what they are, how they happened or how to sort them. To help the reader, I will try to categorize stains into types and then work out what the best treatment might be.

Don't get me wrong, many stains have given me the runaround, especially those that are old, are well washed in, or I have no idea what they are, but I tend to get there in the end. So that you don't end up taking forever to sort out a problem, as I so often have, I hope to be able to guide and direct as follows by detailing further those stains that have not so far been covered in my other books.

I think the most challenging stain problem for me was a large black mark on a dark red cotton pair of men's shorts. Where to begin? I had no idea what it was. The shorts had already been washed, yet it had remained. It could be oil, I thought, so I went to 'fatty stains' and wet the stain, massaged in the bicarb and washing-up liquid paste, popped the shorts in a bag overnight so the paste didn't dry out, then washed them the next day. Still there . . .

Next, I soaked them in a Pure Magic and cold water

solution, then left them to drip-dry outside in full sunshine without rinsing. In fact, I left them out for several days, come rain or shine. Still there . . .

Washing soda and green bleach soak overnight then a 20°C long eco wash. Still there . . .

There was no way these shorts could be worn with this huge stain on them, so I decided on my 'when all else fails' remedy. The dark red shorts went into a bowl, I sprinkled over 2 teaspoons of green bleach, poured over just-boiled water to cover, poked them into the solution using a wooden spoon (which got a welcome clean at the same time!) and left them for 4 hours.

The stain was gone! The colour of the shorts hadn't changed at all, the shorts hadn't shrunk, and it was at this point I realized green bleach could be safely used on colours – but not as a first treatment.

I am often asked, how do I know what to use where? Below is a 'where to start' step-by-step guide, and of course it is much easier if you know what the stain is.

Acidic Stains

These include fruit and vegetable stains, curry, juice, grass stains and wine.

Add 2 tablespoons of Pure Magic (see page 12) to a large bowl of cold water and soak for half an hour, then leave the item to drip-dry outside, without rinsing, in full sunshine or bright daylight. For a full version of this tip, see page 69.

Fatty Stains

These include grease, butter, oil, chocolate, make-up, sun cream and fake tan.

Mix a thin paste made from 2–3 teaspoons of bicarbonate of soda and a squirt of eco-friendly washing-up liquid. Wet the stain lightly using water in a spray bottle then massage in the paste, putting plenty on. Pop the item in a plastic bag overnight so the paste doesn't dry out, then wash the next day in a 20°C long eco wash. Whether the stain is fresh or already washed in, this method works well.

Sticky Stains

These include glue, tree sap, beeswax, chewing gum, biro, nail varnish and some inks.

Use a cotton pad dipped in surgical spirit to dab at stains caused by the above, whether on clothing, furniture or carpets. The alcohol quickly evaporates and shouldn't leave a mark. This is an on-the-spot treatment; for the full method see page 67.

Bloodstains

Bloodstains are easier to remove when fresh than when they have dried in. Either way, cold salt water I find works the best. Use a ratio of 50g (1¾oz) salt dissolved in 250ml (8fl oz) hot water, then leave until cold. If you decide to cook boiled eggs in the microwave (see page 230) then save the cooking water in a bottle so that you are ready to tackle any bloodstains. Use the solution to either soak stained clothing or dab with a cloth to remove from furniture, carpets or mattresses. Try to remember that slowly does it – dab, don't rub, and never overwet carpets or furniture. In short, a cold, salt-water soak for clothing and dabbing for furniture and carpets.

Persistent Stains after Washing or Treatment

This is for ink, whiteboard marker, crayons, paint and any stain that refuses to comply!

Make up a concentrated green bleach solution and, using an artist's paintbrush, brush the stain at regular intervals until the stain dissolves – see full method on page 119.

General Dirt, Stubborn Stains, Odours and Grubbiness

This includes sweat and body odour, mud, everyday work clothes, sports kits, etc., and – as so often happens – those stains missed on the first wash.

I find a tepid overnight in washing soda works wonders. In a washing-up bowl add 2-3 tablespoons washing soda and 1 teaspoon green bleach (for whites and colours), pour in about 500ml boiling water and stir until dissolved. Add cold water to cool it down to tepid, then soak the items overnight. Next day, wring them out and wash as normal on a long 20°C eco cycle.

Absolutely Impossible

This always happens. There is a stain, you've no idea what the stain is and will happily do anything to try and sort it out. You have tried everything: washing soda, Pure Magic, sunshine, tepid soaks, cold washing. On these occasions I decide that if it is an item I cannot wear again in its present state, I give it the hot treatment. See page 60 for my story about a pair of dark red shorts that gave me the runaround – following this method, I finally conquered the stain without any adverse effect on the colour.

Pop the item into a bowl, sprinkle over 2 teaspoons green bleach and pour over boiling water to cover. Use a wooden spoon to keep the item submerged below the waterline and even lay a plate over the top if necessary. Soak for 3–4 hours (the bleach becomes inactive after this time), then rinse and keep fingers crossed. This method has worked for me more times than it hasn't.

COLOUR RUN

I have lost count of the number of crisis calls for help due to colour runs. It may be that colour has run from a shirt into a white collar, a coloured sock has tinted the white items in the load, or white stripes have greyed over time on a much-loved garment. My solution here may not fix every problem every time, or on the first try, and in the end some garments cannot be returned to their former glory because some dyes refuse to budge, yet equally there have been many success stories.

First, prevention is better than cure. If you have a brand new garment that's never been washed, with maybe a white stripe or white collar and the rest is coloured, then to prevent a future problem a cold soak overnight before you first wash it, using one part vinegar to two parts water, should fix the dye and avoid any colour runs. Cold washing will also prevent colour runs.

If the colour has run, first try this treatment. Add 2 teaspoons of green bleach to a bowl just big enough to take the item, then pour over a little just-boiled water to activate. Stir, then once dissolved add sufficient cold water to take the temperature to tepid. Add the garment and leave for 3–4 hours. Hopefully the white has whitened and the colour tint has disappeared.

Sometimes, following this first treatment, it appears the item has changed colour completely – maybe gone from a dye-stained pink and now to grey! It should be white. In this situation, repeat the treatment, only this time don't cool down the temperature of the soaking liquid – leave it hand hot. After dissolving the green bleach in boiling water, add the now-grey item and this time it should bleach white in 3–4 hours of soaking.

TOUGH STICKY STAINS

Chewing gum, glue, tree sap, fresh ink, biro, lipstick, spots and paint splashes. We've all seen it happen, and always at the worst moment! There are too many incidences to recall when I have been put on the spot, and this is my first go-to, whatever the fabric – whether it be clothing, soft furnishings, car seats, carpets, you name it.

You will need

small bowl (if appropriate)
old towel or tea towel
cotton pad

surgical spirit

If the disaster has struck on a piece of clothing, you will need to upturn the bowl on a work surface, then cover it with the old towel or tea towel and place the stain on the towel.

Soak the small cotton pad (I use a reusable make-up remover pad) in surgical spirit then begin to dab at the stain from the wrong side of the fabric. Lipstick, some (non-permanent) biro and ink stains, spots and splashes will then transfer from the garment onto the towel below. Keep moving the towel underneath so that the stain doesn't transfer back onto the garment.

When it comes to glue, tree sap, paint and chewing gum, use the bowl as a firm area to work on, but have the stain uppermost. Again, dab at the mark and eventually the alcohol should dissolve the offending stain. When it comes to chewing gum, a large blob can be removed first by popping the garment into the freezer for a few hours. The frozen gum can then be pulled off in a single piece, leaving maybe a few stubborn strands which can be dissolved with the surgical spirit.

This method even worked for me on a washed-in foundation make-up stain on a pair of my granddaughter's black leggings and a very old chewing gum stain which had turned black and had defaced a pair of cream stretch leggings. I stretched the leggings over the bowl with the stain uppermost and after a few dabs – problem solved.

Tree sap, the thick, brown, gluey substance, again responded well to this treatment, even after I had washed the item. Followers have removed Blu Tack, slime and nail varnish from carpets using this method, so I urge you to give this a try before dashing out for expensive and harmful solvents, sprays and stain removers.

Slime-stained clothing can be remedied using an overnight soak in 2–3 tablespoons of washing soda dissolved in hot water that's been cooled to tepid, before washing the next day.

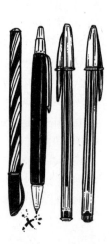

REMOVE A CURRY STAIN
FROM A WHITE T-SHIRT

Even worse, how do I remove curry, chilli, tomato sauce, turmeric, mustard and blackcurrant stains that remain after washing? As with any fruit or veg stains, pre-soaking with a simple vinegar and cold water solution as soon as possible should do much to eradicate the stain before washing. Rinse off as much of the stain as possible under the cold tap, then combine one part vinegar to two parts water in a bowl and soak the t-shirt overnight. However, and it is easily done, sometimes the stain is missed, goes into the washing machine along with other soiled items and, lo and behold, it is still present. In this case, there's no need to buy proprietary stain-removing products, just try this blend.

You will need

medium mixing bowl
sunny day

2–3 tbsp Pure Magic (see page 12)
500–600ml (17–20fl oz) cold water

Add the measure of Pure Magic to the bowl with the cold water, then add the t-shirt or garment. Soak for half an hour or so, then take it outside, hang it on the line and leave to drip-dry. A sunny day will give quicker results, though simple daylight will also work. Once the garment has dried, take a look and hopefully the stain has disappeared. If the stain was strong or had been fixed in through washing, there may still be traces. If so, move on to the next stage.

Take the bowl and turn it upside down. Position the shirt in such a way that the stain sits across the base of the bowl and the remainder of the shirt can be tucked under and into the hollow of the bowl. Pull the t-shirt and stain taut, then spray Pure Magic directly onto the stain. Massage in with the fingers then leave on a bright sunny windowsill, or better still outside in full direct sunlight. Check regularly, though usually a day outside in the sun or 2–3 days on a windowsill is sufficient to ensure the stain is eradicated.

Wash the garment, dry, and all trace of stains will be gone.

Many followers use Pure Magic and sunshine to whiten and brighten reusable fabric nappies. Even strong sunshine on its own will do a fantastic natural bleaching of certain stains. I remember a pale blue cotton shirt coming out of the washing machine with a tomato stain still well evident. I was in a rush, didn't have the time or patience to give it extra treatment, vowing to sort it later. Absolutely no need. I left it out in the sunshine – stain gone.

REMOVE PRINTER INK FROM
A PURE WOOL CABLE SWEATER

When a mishap happened while changing a printer cartridge, which resulted in a thick blob of black printer ink right in the centre front of a pale grey, 100 per cent wool cable sweater, I was not sure what to do or if it would ever come out. The ink had dried but it hadn't gone through to the inside.

I decided to apply my method where I lay an old towel over a bowl, put the ink stain onto the towel and dab at it from the underside, so that hopefully it would transfer onto the towel. Unfortunately, nothing went to plan – the ink didn't transfer onto the towel but instead spread even further into the wool and transferred also to the inside of the jumper. What was a black blob about ½cm (¼in) wide was now slightly paled but spread to about 2.5cm (1in) in diameter. I had actually made it much worse.

This jumper had been expensive, too, but before giving up I decided to try using Pure Magic. I had never used it on wool before, fearing it might bleach out the colour, but on this occasion, I really didn't have anything to lose. I gingerly used an artist's paintbrush to carefully paint only onto the ink stain, then left the jumper lying over an upturned bowl on the sunny windowsill in the conservatory. I left it for a week – inspecting it daily and re-painting the ink as I could see it was starting to fade.

The outcome? The ink is no longer visible, there is a very pale area that I know about, but all in all the jumper is now stain-free. When I am asked whether Pure Magic is safe to use on wool my reply has to be as a last resort – try always a tepid overnight soak in home-made detergent first (see page 52). Add 100ml (3½fl oz) detergent to a bowl, pour over hot water, swish around, then top up with cold until tepid before adding the woollen garment. Leave to soak, well submerged, overnight, then hand-wash the next day.

Natural wool is very good at releasing stains, and only if you are really stuck should you be prepared to use Pure Magic or green bleach and a paintbrush.

CLEAN REUSABLE MAKE-UP PADS
AND COTTON FLANNELS

I bought a pack of these almost at the start of my green journey and they are still in use. I have added to them and now have quite a pile, but I save them up and wash them together every couple of weeks. When they become threadbare they move onto my cleaning shelf to be used to dab on surgical spirit for removing stains, etc. (see page 67) – and when they finally give up being useful indoors, I pop them onto the compost pile to end their life ultimately on my veggie plot outdoors.

I have to say I like my reusable make-up pads and cotton flannels to be 'whiter than white'. Even though they may have been washed, if they are stained or discoloured they don't feel right and certainly don't look like a successful green swap. This solution works to clean up to 20 heavily soiled make-up pads and 2 cotton flannels.

You will need

medium mixing bowl
just-boiled water
wooden fork or spoon
saucers or side plate, to cover
zip-up laundry bag

3 tbsp washing soda
2 tsp green bleach

Measure the washing soda and green bleach into the bowl, add in the soiled make-up pads and top with 2 folded off-colour cotton flannels. Pour over sufficient just-boiled water to cover everything, then fill to within about 5cm (2in) of the top of the bowl with cold water.

The items will float to begin with, so I use a wooden spoon or fork to gently push them down (as an added benefit, any staining to your wooden spoon or fork will bleach clean). The solution will then begin to foam as the bleach is activated and the soda crystals dissolve, and at that point I lay the saucer or plate over to ensure every pad is submerged. Leave overnight.

The next day, remove the items from the bowl and squeeze out any excess water, then transfer the make-up pads to the zip-up laundry bag – so they don't scatter everywhere amongst your laundry, only to be found stuck in the rubber seal, or get completely lost and then be discovered later hidden in the corner of a pillow case! The flannels can stay loose. Pop both into the drum of the washing machine along with the rest of the whites/lights load and run a long eco cold wash at 20°C. The pads and flannels will be bright white after washing.

TIP: If you have an AGA, add the soiled items, 2 tablespoons washing soda and 1 teaspoon green bleach to a large casserole dish with a well-fitting lid. Pour over water until the pan is three-quarters full, cover and place in the low (simmering) oven overnight. The next morning the cloths etc will be bleached clean and ready to wash as above.

WEDDING DRESS CLEAN

A follower once messaged me to ask how she should wash a wedding dress! I was sent screenshots of the said dress, which was no longer white but grey and was described by the follower as 'absolutely filthy'. The weather had been wet on her wedding day, and the train of the dress had mopped up so much dirt it really did look a lost cause. The quote from the dry cleaners was exorbitant, and even then a disclaimer was thrown in stating that a thorough clean wasn't to be guaranteed. With my guidance, she decided to do it herself.

Sometime later I had a fantastic opportunity to clean a five-layer dress myself following a family wedding – satin, lace, sequins – and as well as the dress there was the veil. It too had been a wet day, so the bottom of the dress was badly stained, but I couldn't wait to get going.

You will need

bath
hot water
cold water

500g washing soda
4 tsp green bleach

TO MACHINE WASH, IF NECESSARY:
single duvet cover

2–3 tbsp washing soda
100ml (3½fl oz) home-made detergent (see page 52) or use
    2–3 tbsp powder detergent (see page 58)

Start by adding the washing soda and green bleach to the bath, then pour on very hot water in order to dissolve the washing soda and activate the bleach. Once dissolved, add sufficient cold water to bring the bath water to about one-third full and make the water temperature tepid – neither hot nor cold. Lay the dress into the tepid solution in one layer and leave to soak overnight.

The next day, if the dress hadn't been too badly soiled it may only need a cold rinse then a very short spin in the washing machine and to be air-dried. If, like this dress, the garment had been very soiled, empty the bath water and if it is mud-coloured, repeat the soak. The next day, rinse the dress by popping the plug into the bath and filling it with cold water. Rinse the dress and then – as best you can without wringing it – gently squeeze any excess water from the dress and pop it inside a single duvet cover, as this will act as a huge, protective laundry bag for the beads, sequins, etc.

Wash the dress inside the duvet cover at just 20°C using 2–3 tablespoons of washing soda in the detergent drawer and 100ml (3½fl oz) of home-made detergent or 2–3 tbsp powder detergent, or your non-biological eco detergent of choice. Finish with just the shortest of spins to remove excess moisture, then place on a dress hanger and leave to air-dry.

After seeing the incredible before and after pictures, many others went on to wash their wedding dresses at home with gorgeous results – saving the planet and money. I have had followers too who have washed vintage christening gowns and baby clothes in the same way, and often just the soak then a hand-wash is sufficient – no need for a machine wash.

STINKY SECOND-HAND
CLOTHES AND FURNITURE

I love a bargain, and I feel recycling, upcycling, buying second-hand and vintage clothing and furniture is a fantastic way to reduce waste, save money and help the planet. A second-hand item bought online, from a charity shop or antique shop may just fit the bill – until you get it home!

A piece of furniture, say an upholstered chair or chest of drawers, once they have taken up residence in your house may begin to permeate tobacco smells or fusty odours. A family member of mine bought a huge second-hand bean bag for her teenage son's bedroom but couldn't believe it when the awful smell from it filled the whole of the upstairs! Similarly, I have had so many messages from followers who have bought items of clothing second-hand or have taken old clothing out of storage to find it to be fusty smelling and really not fit to wear.

The initial reaction is often to spray all over the garment or piece of furniture with perfume or air freshener, but this can often make the problem worse and add to the odour rather than masking it. Our hero, bicarbonate of soda, is amongst its many uses also a fantastic odour neutralizer.

You will need

sugar shaker filled with bicarbonate of soda
dried lavender (optional)

large reusable 'bag for life' (I know we hate plastic, and I am
   working on an alternative, but for now we can use the
   same one over and over)

For upholstered and wooden items

Dust them all over with bicarbonate of soda. The lavender is
optional, but it will perfume the bicarb to make the whole
operation slightly more pleasing. It is important that the item
being treated is dry, so if it is damp at all, leave it in a warm
room for a day before sprinkling over the bicarb. Once sprinkled (and don't be afraid to put plenty on), leave in a roomy
warm space for a day or two. You should notice that when you
walk into the room the odour is neutralized, and if you use
lavender the smell is pleasing and fresh. Brush off excess
powder, then vacuum up the rest, and your previously malodorous item can take on the nicer smells in your house.

For dry-clean-only dresses and jackets

I turn these inside out before dusting over the bicarb – especially on dark colours. Small items such as soft toys and
handbags can be dusted over, too. Pop them into the large
plastic bag or similar and leave in a warm place for a day or
two. Take the bag outside and give the items a shake and a
brush – or shake them over the bath or in a shower cubicle if
there is no outdoor space. Clothing can be given a good shake
then turned to the right side, then I often simply hang them
on a clothes hanger outside for an hour or two to blow in the
fresh air, or in an airy room indoors.

Washable items

Stinky items that are washable can be either soaked overnight in a tepid washing soda solution or sprayed with vinegar and washed straight away – I have found either way to be effective.

Washing soda soak

Dissolve 2–3 tablespoons of washing soda in very hot water in a medium sink or large bowl, let the water cool down to tepid, then add the garment and soak overnight. This is best suited to woollens and silks and those items you prefer to hand-wash rather than put in the machine. Next day, hand-wash in tepid water using 50ml (1¾fl oz) home-made detergent (see page 52).

Vinegar spray

I always have a spray bottle filled with white vinegar, which is a handy stain and odour treatment when in a hurry and there's no time for an overnight soak. For fusty and smelly clothes, evidence of a stain or a sweat mark – a good spray 30 minutes or so before popping them into the washing machine can help to dissolve stains and eliminate odours.

DRY-ISH CLEANING OF PILLOWS, MATTRESSES, QUILTS AND STUBBORN CARPET AND UPHOLSTERY STAINS

Pillows, quilts, mattresses, carpets and soft furnishings take their fair share of stains, whether from perspiration, bed-wetting accidents, spilt drinks, or general dirt from everyday living – it happens. Replacing soiled items is expensive, as is dry cleaning or bringing in the experts.

My kitchen carpet (more a rug than a carpet) was very badly stained. I had tried spot cleaning as well as an overall clean on my hands and knees, but I could never quite get it right until I put together this simple recipe, which has since gone on to be a real favourite with followers, cleaning up mattresses, pillows, and stubborn upholstery and carpet stains when all else has failed.

MAKES SUFFICIENT TO CLEAN A LARGE RUG,
MATTRESS OR 4 PILLOWS

You will need

large bowl
wooden spoon
shower puff
old, clean towel

4 tbsp washing soda
2 tsp green bleach

100ml (3½fl oz) just-boiled water
150ml (5fl oz) cold water
20ml (¾fl oz) eco-friendly washing-up liquid
sugar shaker filled with bicarbonate of soda, for tough areas

Add the washing soda and green bleach to the bowl, pour over the just-boiled water and stir with a spoon until dissolved and beginning to foam. Then add the cold water and washing-up liquid. Use the shower puff to work at the mix until the bowl is filled with suds.

Using the shower puff and the washing soda and green bleach mix, work in sections on large areas like mattresses, carpets and upholstery, massaging over a layer of suds. Any stains and difficult areas can be first given a sprinkle of bicarbonate of soda to help with the cleaning. Immediately after one section is complete, wipe over with the towel so that the area doesn't become too wet, then move on to the next bit.

Pillows can be done outside on a sunny day and then left in the sunshine to whiten and brighten.

When working on very dark fabrics, use just half a teaspoon of green bleach.

KITCHEN RESCUE!

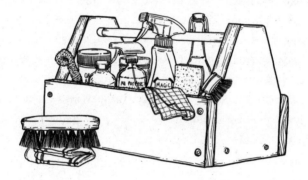

This chapter does what it says and will rescue those kitchen items or situations where you maybe thought the only way was to the bin!

A kitchen rescue is so satisfying and one you always want to share with your friends, because not only did you save the day, you saved money too! The burnt pan, a rusty tin, keeping flour safe, resolving 'sticky' issues – there is almost always a fix. As with any tip – once you know it and have used it – you will never forget, and I am always hungry and eager to find new ways to solve problems.

BURNT PANS, COOKING POTS
AND TRAYS

I don't think a day goes by that I am not sent a message about accidental burnt-on rice pudding, milk, curry, stews, jams (the worst) and soups, just to mention a few. This is an effortless overnight treatment that will clean up even the most burnt or dried- and baked-on food deposits in pans, bowls and dishes, with a variant for aluminium baking trays.

You will need

a sink or bowl large enough to submerge the item
fine wire wool or a scrunched-up piece of aluminium foil

3–4 tbsp washing soda
just-boiled water
1 tbsp bicarbonate of soda
1–2 tsp green bleach (for aluminium items)

Place the burnt vessel in the bowl or sink, sprinkle over the washing soda then pour over sufficient just-boiled water to cover. Leave overnight to soak. The next day, simply wipe away the softened debris, and any remaining stubborn parts can be easily cleaned using dampened fine wire wool or scrunched-up foil dipped into dry bicarbonate of soda.

Aluminium should not be soaked using washing soda as the metal permanently tarnishes. Instead, leave to soak in a green bleach solution of 1–2 teaspoons of green bleach and boiling water – it does a sterling job on grease-stained, aluminium cooker-hood filters.

Burnt-on sugar and jams can be even more troublesome and can successfully glue a spoon to the base of the pan while cooking, too. The washing soda soak above will work, but in order to remove the thickest layer of burnt sugar or jam you need to first fill the pan with water and slowly heat it on the hob. The sugar will dissolve, any stuck spoon will unstick and the pan will be cleaned of the thickest of the mess. Discard the sugary water, then add the washing soda and just-boiled water as above and leave to soak overnight. Next day, a light rub with a cloth, or at worst a rub with wire wool dipped in bicarb, and all will be gleaming again.

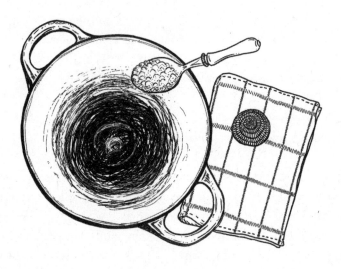

TIP: I'll add just a little tip here particularly for Aga owners or those whose oven is on low and maybe has sufficient space. I had a very badly burnt casserole pan (not a large one) and I had done a proper job on it. It was late at night and I knew I should leave it to soak overnight. This was an enamel casserole and just on a whim I decided instead to add a teaspoon washing soda, a teaspoon green bleach, fill with cold water and on with the lid and into my low simmering oven and left it overnight. Next day – you guessed it – I took off the lid and the water inside was steaming and dark brown. The burnt on deposits were completely gone and the pan cleaner than it had ever been, clean while you sleep!

LIFETIME PANS: RENEW AND REVIVE CAST IRON

I have a treasured cast-iron frying pan that has been in my kitchen forever – I don't even recall where it came from, though it is at least forty-five years old. It is a small one, perfect for pancakes and crêpes, for frying a couple of eggs – it is so beautiful and I love it. It has been in use for so many years, is well seasoned and therefore food usually doesn't stick to it.

When I say 'well seasoned', this doesn't mean it has been impregnated with herbs and spices, it is the term given to a cast-iron pan that has been coated with a thin layer of oil and then heated in the oven at a high temperature for half an hour. Well-used pans eventually become so well seasoned that in the end they are covered with a natural non-stick coating that will also protect them from rusting. Unlike most modern non-stick coatings, which are fine when the pan is new but eventually scratch and, at worst, flake off into food. I doubt any of my non-stick-coated pans will stand the test of time.

For this reason I am always on the lookout for a bargain cast-iron buy. I have a large cast-iron casserole pan – huge – which I picked up for a song because it was badly rusted and clearly neglected, I got to work.

You will need

2 tbsp washing soda
Sufficient boiling water to fill the pot or pan

Pure Magic (see page 12)
1 tbsp coconut oil (and additional oil for a second or third
'seasoning')

I started with an overnight soak in 2 tablespoons of washing
soda and boiling water, then the next day gave it a good clean
and dried it thoroughly by leaving it outside in the fresh air.
The pan looked clean yet dull, mottled and grey in colour, and
I still had a few rust spots.

A spray of Pure Magic quickly dissolved the rust, then I
washed the pan in clean water and left it outside to dry again
in the fresh air. Next, I melted 1 tablespoon of coconut oil in
a bowl in the microwave for just 5 seconds, then rubbed it all
over the casserole pan. You can use any oil, but I favour coconut
oil due to its anti-bacterial qualities. To finish the 'seasoning'
of my newly acquired treasure, I waited for the oven to go on
for my next loaf of bread (hot oven, 230°C/210°C fan/450°F/
gas 8) and popped the casserole pan in for half an hour at the
same time. The oil seals to a non-stick coat, which not only
enhances the appearance of the cast iron but also prevents any
future rust.

If you invest in a brand new piece of cast-iron cookware
the manufacturers will have most likely seasoned it slightly,
though I now season mine a further two times before using.

It is worth taking the time to do this because when done
at the outset the non-stick benefit will be there always, and
in fact will be ameliorated with every use.

This seasoning of cookware can also be extended to bakeware.
My Yorkshire pudding tin is blackened with layers and layers
of hot oil 'seasoning'. I never wash it and it never sticks. Just
a wipe with a damp cloth after each use.

STUCK-FAST CROCKERY AND GLASSES

If this has ever happened to you, you will remember it. Either in the cupboard, while washing up or simply stacking, you find that two identical glass bowls, jugs or tumblers get themselves stuck together and no matter how hard you try pulling this way, twisting that way, they won't come apart.

I have friends tell me that the only way to separate them is to bang one against a hard surface and the other will be freed, but this is very high risk and can easily result in a glass or bowl getting smashed. This method is much more successful.

You will need

ice cubes or a bag of frozen peas
warm water in the sink (use hot water for Pyrex, it won't
   crack)

Take your two stuck bowls, glasses or jugs and stand the bottom one in the sink of warm water, then add the ice cubes or bag of frozen peas into the top one. After a minute or so they will separate effortlessly. The icy cold of the top item causes the bowl or glass to contract, while the heat from the water around the bottom item causes it to expand and, hey-ho – sorted! Pop the peas (if using) back into the freezer.

REMOVE ODOURS AND STAINS
FROM FLASKS AND PLASTIC
WATER BOTTLES

This query crops up very often, as many more people rightly opt for reusable water and drinking bottles rather than a single-use bottle of water. Similarly, the much-loved Thermos flask can get stained and smelly, especially when not cleaned and dried thoroughly after use, and even more so if stored with the cap on.

With regular use our reusable drinking vessels can become pretty unsightly, smelly and even grow mould. Rather than having to go to the expense of renewing them regularly, try to get into a cleaning routine and your reusables will continue to be so for a long time. I am thinking especially of children's bottles that spend a day at school and can come back as grubby as the child itself. This is a good daily routine for any much-loved and -used item.

You will need

1 tsp washing soda
½ tsp green bleach
just-boiled water

Add the above measures to each flask and bottle you want to treat, top up with just-boiled water right to the rim and leave to soak overnight. Next day, rinse thoroughly to clean and neutralize any odours. Always store flasks and water bottles without the cap so that air can circulate, which prevents odours and mould developing.

REMOVE FOOD STAINS AND ODOURS FROM PLASTIC STORAGE CONTAINERS AND BLENDERS

Certain foods can stain storage containers and plastic blender cups. Bolognese sauces, curry sauces, soups and stews may leave an orange tinge in the plastic boxes that have been used for freezer or fridge storage. When ordinary washing didn't clean them up I used to reach for a bottle of harmful chlorine bleach, but not any more.

Quick and easy: simply spray a couple of squirts of Pure Magic (see page 12) directly into the stained item, then rub it around the container with your hands or a sink brush, adding in a couple of tablespoons of water, if necessary, to make it go further. Leave for 10 minutes, or longer if the stains are very dark, then wash thoroughly once you see the staining has gone.

CLEAN PLASTIC CHOPPING BOARDS

Many homes have them, some colour-coded to help prevent confusion and cross-contamination: red for meat, green for veggies, yellow for chicken, blue for fish, and white, presumably, for bread. With the best will in the world, they do stain – and in my house the green veggie and white boards seem to stain the most. Even when not visibly grubby, it is recommended they be given a regular clean to sanitize them, remove odours and any residual staining. Rather than reaching for harmful chlorine bleach, we can clean and sanitize without harming the environment.

You will need

sink or large bowl
small but heavy bowl or jug
sink brush
bright daylight

2–3 tbsp washing soda
2 tsp green bleach
just-boiled water
Pure Magic spray (see page 12)

Lay the stained board in the sink or a bowl large enough so that it can lie flat, then sprinkle over the washing soda and green bleach. Pour over the just-boiled water to about 5cm (2in) deep. The board, being plastic, will float, so stand a heavy bowl or jug on top to weigh it down. Leave for several hours or overnight, then take out of the solution. Scrub the board with the sink brush and the board will be clean and any odours gone.

Grooves made by cutting lines on plastic boards can be stubborn and appear to still be badly stained, but give them a quick spray with Pure Magic, then don't rinse it off but stand the board outside in full sun or daylight – even a sunny windowsill will work – and any residual marks will disappear.

Pure Magic does dry leaving a sticky residue, so rinse the board with warm water before using. If the staining is not too bad, Pure Magic may not even be necessary – placing the wet boards outside in the sun will bleach the stains for free.

AVOID DOMES AND CRACKS ON CAKES

For tray bakes where you want even-sized pieces, not skinny ones from the sides and fat ones from the centre, it is important that the finished bake has a flat top. Not only will every slice be uniform in size, I know that I can pour over a topping that will give an even layer and not pool around the edges due to a dome or, at worst, begin to infill a huge crack in the centre.

A crack and dome is not always a bad thing, by the way. In fact, for some cakes, particularly loaf cakes, a crack down the centre is very attractive – but everything has its place! A dome or crack is usually caused by either the oven temperature being a little too hot, the oven maybe having hot spots, or the tin being of a certain thickness or type that has conducted the heat quickly. Cake heat diffusers are available to buy – usually lengths of sponge-type material that are dampened then wrapped around the tins before baking. We can make our own for a fraction of the price, and unlike the manufactured equivalents (which are often constructed from a man-made plastic foam), these can be recycled once they have been used so many times that they have become weak and fragile.

All you need is a collar made from aluminium foil, and I use my collars over and over until they eventually tear. As the foil hasn't been contaminated by food I can happily add them to my metal recycling bin. To make a collar, cut a length of foil long enough to fit right around the sides of your tin with an extra 10cm (4in) at the end. Fold the foil in half lengthways and cut into two. A double thickness of foil is sufficient so fold each piece lengthways again, making two collars. You can join the collars together to make one large piece to surround a large tray-bake tin or use them separately for a couple of sandwich cakes.

After filling your tin or tins with cake batter, wrap a foil collar around the outside of the tin and pinch the ends together to secure using the 10cm (4in) overlap. Bake as normal – the foil will diffuse the oven's heat, ensuring a gentle, even bake that avoids a dome or crack, so that each slice of your finished tray bake will be the same size.

STORE-CUPBOARD STAPLES

I am lucky to have a pantry next to my kitchen and I love it. I have shelves for my preserved chutneys, marmalade, jams and pickles on one side. On the other side I have tins, jars, spices, rice, pasta and those everyday sauces and condiments that can be called upon at any time to complete a recipe. It is an Aladdin's cave of food treasures.

We all have a collection of store-cupboard staples that we tend to think will last forever – and some do. For example, salt and honey have an indefinite shelf life, which I find amazing, and technically sugar never spoils and vinegar doesn't expire. There are other foods of course, and particularly dried foods, which will last a very long time – pasta, white rice, dried beans and pulses usually have at least a two-year expiry date that I would happily push on a few months as long as it still looked and smelt fine. Brown rice doesn't last as long however, and can discolour, smell rancid and have an oily texture after just a few months.

Canned foods are brilliant too and will last a very long time as long as the tin itself is not damaged or rusted. Just because a cupboard staple may have expired and lost its pungency or strength doesn't mean it cannot be used or reused.

Keep Your Flour Safe

For those readers who rarely bake, a bag of flour may be a rare purchase. I remember many years ago I had a very small dark kitchen which was very humid, with little in the way of shelf space, and I had a bag of flour which had somehow found itself at the back of the cupboard and had not been disturbed in probably months. In those days there were no 'sell by' or 'use by' dates and if food had a pleasing smell then it was fine to eat. I still do this, by the way – rather than be governed by supermarket dates on goods.

Anyway, back to the flour – I opened the bag to make Yorkshire puddings to see tiny, creepy weevils or flour mites busying around inside. I was shocked. How did they get in there?

Apparently weevils can sometimes survive the milling process and eggs can hatch into the flour, but more often they find a way into the paper bag of flour themselves, the female laying her eggs for the youngsters to then hatch later.

I remember my grandmother telling me to sieve them out – they'll not cause any harm – and that was one of the reasons why sieving of flour used to be carried out back in the day. I was totally put off by them and the flour was tossed into the bin. Flour weevils are not harmful or poisonous, but prevention is better than cure, so if you use flour rarely it is worth keeping it in an airtight glass jar, plastic tub or tin with a well-fitting lid. If you do encounter flour weevils and really don't fancy eating the flour, even after sifting, it can be safely composted – paper bag too.

Reuse Your Oil

Cooking oil from deep- or shallow-frying can be reused. To keep it in good shape, I like to strain it to remove food remnants such as blackened, burnt breadcrumbs or frizzled batter. I will reuse my oil three or four times before discarding it as directed by the local council's advice (you can't pour oil down the sink).

You will need

plastic funnel
bottle with lid for storage
absorbent kitchen paper or paper coffee filter
tea strainer or little sieve

Allow the used cooking oil to cool completely.

Place the funnel into the neck of the bottle and line it with paper – a paper coffee filter is perfect for this, but if you don't have one you can make your own from a single sheet of absorbent kitchen paper. Take one sheet, fold it in half and then in half again so that the sheet is a quarter of its original size. Peel back one of the four openings so that you have a cone shape and slot that into the neck of the funnel.

I also like to pour the oil through a tea strainer and then through the paper and down the funnel into the bottle. The strained oil will be crystal clear and can be used at least three or four times more. If in doubt about how many times to use your oil, if it discolours or has an unpleasant smell, don't use it again.

Expired Herbs and Spices

Just because your herbs and spices may have best-before dates doesn't mean they are not fit for use. Dried herbs and spices simply lose their pungency after time. I use mine way beyond the dates stated on their jars, though once I consider they have had their day I either add the contents to the compost bin and reuse the jars or sprinkle them around my vegetable beds, as they can be an effective deterrent to insects and small animals. One sniff of ground cinnamon and they're off!

Cinnamon is also a great rooting powder for cuttings as it prohibits mould growth, so move your expired jar from the kitchen out into the potting shed and you won't need to purchase a tub of proprietary rooting mix.

Expired Oils

When I clear out my pantry and give things a sort out, moving older foods to the front, etc., I am not usually too fussed about best-before dates, especially on tinned and dried foods. My rule of thumb is usually to check the smell. Certain oils can smell rancid when they are out of date, and I recall a small bottle of truffle oil that I paid a fortune for on holiday, then hardly ever used, smelling pretty rough when I unscrewed the cap. As it was only a small bottle, rather than sending it to the council tip (there is an oil recycling bin there), I instead decided to keep it in the garden shed to rub over my garden tools to prevent them rusting up.

PLAIN FLOUR

CAN I REUSE FREEZER BAGS?

Freezer bags used for meat, eggs and fish I use just the one time, but others that have been used for cheese, vegetables, bread, crumble mix, pesto cubes, etc., I wash and reuse. Sometimes even after washing it may be that I can still detect the smell of the food – raspberries, for example, leave an odour (though not unpleasant), as do frozen peppers and pesto. After washing, I turn the bag inside out and peg it outside for a day or two, whatever the weather. Any odour will then disappear.

I don't reuse plastic freezer bags for ever and ever, and once I see that they no longer look fit for purpose, have developed a tear or hole or look dull, I discard them. I am gradually changing up to plastic sealed freezer boxes and glass jars that have a much longer shelf life and can be used over and over.

Glass jars freeze well, but if you are using them always leave expansion space at the top – don't fill them to the brim.

HOME HACKS

E veryday tips and tricks can rapidly turn a sigh into a smile. A quick and easy, no-cost yet smarter way to do this or that and at the same time achieve the same result is what makes me happy. I love a 'two-in-one' fix for something, or to discover I needn't use as much of something to get the same result. All of the tips coming up in this chapter have at some time or another been really helpful to me and I wonder sometimes how I first got to know some of them. As you read through you will probably recognize some if not all of the problems – you may have little hacks of your own but if not, try these.

STEAMY WINDOWS

Pools of condensation on sills and windows steamed up are indicators that there is lots of moisture in the air. As this vapour hits the cold glass it condenses, the windows steam up, and at worst there are rivers running down the glass. These pools of condensation, if not mopped up, can soak into curtains and blinds, which go mouldy (see page 27). I used to use this little tip in the 1970s before I had central heating, but nowadays, with limited heating being used, my steamy windows are once again an issue.

You will need

kitchen paper or dry absorbent cloth
eco-friendly washing-up liquid

Mop up any condensation present on the glass using a piece of absorbent paper. Then take a slightly dampened cloth or the same slightly damp piece of kitchen paper with just a blob of washing-up liquid and wipe over the glass. This invisible film will prevent the moisture immediately condensing onto the glass and prevent windows steaming up.

I ran a little experiment and discovered this treatment lasted three weeks on my kitchen window. Obviously this doesn't take away the moisture in the air – it is still present, just not making a mess of your windows. Try where and when possible to keep rooms well ventilated to prevent condensation build-up and mould. This tip also works for steamy bathroom mirrors.

WOOD-BURNING STOVES AND FIREPLACES

Wood-burning stoves are popular, more efficient than open coal fires and can look splendid when lit, providing a cosy welcome to the room.

I have a wood-burning stove with a glass door front that can quickly become blackened. There are products available on the market to manage this, many of which contain some pretty hefty chemicals, but I find this free home hack brilliant and eco-friendly.

You will need

cold wood ash
newspaper or used brown packaging paper

To clean the glass, simply scrunch up a piece of dampened newspaper or used brown packaging paper, then dip it into cold wood ash from the fire. Rub this over the glass – you will see it remove any soot and burnt-on deposits – then polish with a second piece of dry paper. When finished, you can throw them both into the grate to burn later. Job sorted!

STONE AND SLATE

Open fires and/or wood-burning stoves stand majestic on natural stone and slate hearths, and some houses have natural stone or slate windowsills too.

Acidic cleaners (my recipes containing lemon juice, vinegar or citric acid) can penetrate the pores of stone, granite and slate, etching away at the surfaces and making the structure very weak and brittle. Many followers have asked me for a natural cleaning product that will remove stains and generally enrich the appearance of these natural materials without damaging them. This is it.

You will need

glass jar with a screwtop lid
spoon
cleaning cloth
soft sink brush

half quantity of cream cleaner (see page 14)
warm soapy water

Apply the cream cleaner to the stone or slate area then dip the soft sink brush in the warm soapy water and brush the cream into the stone or slate. Rub well in then wipe away using the cleaning cloth, rinsing well. Leave to air-dry naturally.

Followers have sent me before and after photos of their

slate and stone surfaces, now rich and clean, but without the use of any abrasive or harmful chemicals. Always try this out on a test area first, though, choosing a spot that's out of the way and less visible.

ERADICATE WASHING MACHINE AND DISHWASHER SMELLS

Where would we be without our automatic washing machines and dishwashers?

They are such fantastic labour-saving devices, and I remember the wonder when I got my first machine just before my son was born, forty-five years ago. Up until then I had used a second-hand tub with a wringer and wash day really did take *all day*.

Our machines do work very hard and we tend to take them for granted, and even abuse them from time to time. Even the cleanest of machines take a battering – the never-ending laundry following a holiday, for example, and we expect the machine to just get on with it. Then there is the continuous on and off of the dishwasher at Christmas.

We are not always perfect, either – someone fails to clean the plates of food debris before the plates go into the machine, or a tissue, pocketful of sweet papers and the odd coin or screw end up in the washing machine.

Maybe only when the washing machine begins to leave marks on the laundry or the dishwasher stinks a bit when the door is open do we begin to stress, or maybe our heavily used machines simply cry out for a clean!

There are dishwasher and washing machine products specially designed for this job, but have you seen the price? On further examination (you know how I love to browse a hazard data sheet) some brands state specifically that they are harmful to aquatic life, with long-lasting effects.

Dishwasher clean

You will need

sink brush or cloth
2 tbsp washing soda (optional, if greasy)
4 tbsp citric acid

Start by removing the filter and basket – usually located at the bottom of the machine – and remove any food debris caught up in there, then rinse the filter well. If it is really greasy, drop it into the sink, add the washing soda and pour over hot water. Leave to soak for 10 minutes, then clean using a sink brush or cloth.

Replace the filter then sprinkle over the citric acid. There's no need to add it to the detergent dispenser, I throw mine straight into the housing. Close the dishwasher door and choose a 60°C cycle. Your dishwasher will be clean, fresh and sparkling.

Washing machine clean

When I first started my green journey this is where I began – with a big overhaul of the washing machine – and consequently this was the first tip in my first green book. Back then my Pure Magic hadn't been truly put to the test and, because I have developed quicker and more effective ways of carrying out this clean, I decided to include this shortcut version of that original tip which includes everything that I have learned over the intervening years, thanks to all the feedback and questions from my followers.

Limescale, soap scum and fabric conditioners (if you use proprietary ones) can take their toll on washing machines, leaving mould and a rough feel to the detergent dispenser, grey sludge around the rubber seal and, at worst, a dank odour when the washing machine is not in use. Grey marks can appear on what should be clean laundry, and again the machine is crying out for a clean. Citric acid alone is not recommended for cleaning washing machines, as it can cause damage to rubber pipes and seals. I have to confess I used citric acid on its own for some time without an issue, though now I neutralize the acid by adding washing soda to the mix, resulting in my own sodium citrate. This is the active ingredient in proprietary products, but our combination costs a lot less.

You will need

an old toothbrush or bottle brush
cleaning cloths

Pure Magic spray (see page 12)
3 tbsp citric acid
3 tbsp washing soda

After removing the detergent drawer, any soap residue, mould particles and rough-feeling glaze left by limescale can be quickly dissolved using a few squirts of Pure Magic spray. Really stubborn scale will have to sit for 20 minutes or so with the mix before washing off. The inside of the housing and in particular the roof (where the water fills) can be reached using a few sprays, an old toothbrush and a warm and damp cleaning cloth; then keep repeating until all is clear and sparkling.

Give a squirt of Pure Magic spray to the rubber seal to

quickly remove soap scum and dirt accumulated in the rubber, then rinse off immediately – any mould spores will be killed off too. Any residual mould stains I have found fade in time as long as the door is left open when not in use.

Remember the filter usually situated near the floor of the machine. Place a lipped baking tray underneath (or the dog's towel) to catch the 300ml (10fl oz) or so of water that will pour out as it is unscrewed. Clean this out thoroughly – I found a button and a nail in mine one time! Then replace the cover.

Add 3 tablespoons of citric acid and 3 tablespoons of washing soda straight into the washing-machine drum and choose a long, eco 60°C cycle. The first time I did this I was shocked at the particles floating around in the water – soap scum and limescale! Then switch off the machine mid-cycle when the water is still hot and the machine is still in washing mode (not cold rinsing). Leave it overnight to descale. The next day, restart the machine to complete the cycle.

Then run a second 60°C cycle without any additional citric acid or washing soda, and you will see that the water is now clean and clear.

||||||||||||||||||||||||||||||||||||||||||||||||||||||||||||||||||||||||||||||||||||||||||||||||||||||||||||||||||||||||||||||||

TIP: When not in use, leave the washing machine door open or ajar (as well as the detergent drawer) and leave the dishwasher door just slightly ajar to allow air to circulate. This is especially important when you go on holiday or away for a time.

||||||||||||||||||||||||||||||||||||||||||||||||||||||||||||||||||||||||||||||||||||||||||||||||||||||||||||||||||||||||||||||||

DEEP-CLEAN THE TOILET SEAT

I have had so many questions about the toilet seat that I felt I must give it a mention. We all have them, they do get stained, and it may be one of those items we don't want to discuss, don't want to admit to being unsightly underneath, and the solution often is to remove it, toss it into landfill and buy a new one. Older-style toilet seats are secured with fixed brackets and are a job to remove, and obviously when the newer style hit the market it was because owners wanted to be able to remove them to clean.

Examine your toilet seat and lift up the seat to see whether it has a push-in release button. I know many followers didn't even know it was there, so if it has never been used before it may be stiff. Press it in and at the same time rock the seat from side to side until it comes away from the clips that secure it to the toilet. Then leave it to soak in a bath or large utility room sink – some followers even use a wheelbarrow sourced specifically for cleaning oven shelves or the toilet seat!

You may be surprised at what is lurking under the toilet seat, so let's go!

You will need

a large sink, wheelbarrow or bath
clean cloths
rubber gloves

100g (3½oz) of washing soda (for a sink or wheelbarrow)
   or 200–300g (7–10½oz) in the bath
Pure Magic spray (see page 12)

Lay the toilet seat plus the attached lid in the utility sink, wheelbarrow or bath, stained side uppermost. Sprinkle over the washing soda, then add hot water until the seat is submerged. Leave to soak overnight, and by the next day any discolouration and staining will have dissolved. Depending on how bad the seat was, you may need to use a cloth to finish off around the rubber stoppers and fasteners. Rinse well, dry, then it is ready to fix back into place.

During the time that the toilet seat is undergoing its soak, it's on with the rubber gloves, a spray of Pure Magic and work on the toilet itself, which is a doddle when the seat is out of the way and there are no awkward nooks and crannies.

If you are wondering whether washing soda alone is effective enough to carry out a thorough 'germ-busting' clean, I believe it does a great job. It's effective in stain removal for laundry, as we know – I use it with every laundry cycle; and it also cleans drains and unblock sinks. I have done much reading and research to understand that it creates a hostile environment for bacteria, and eradicates smells, while at the same time it is a gentle and natural water softener, which is probably why it is already a major ingredient in many proprietary cleaning products. Soda crystals have been used for up to two hundred years and are one of the oldest-known cleaning materials as well as one of the cheapest.

For the toilet seats that do not remove from the toilet with ease and have to be cleaned in situ, the cream cleaner on page 14 will remove staining and marks.

ELIMINATE STATIC CLING

I have a pair of trousers that annoyingly stick to my legs when I have had them on for a time. I must be a sight to behold when I stand up from my chair and the trousers have risen up and are clinging in folds around my legs, leaving my ankles and lower legs bare. I then have to pull down on the trousers to return them to their rightful place!

I already know that vinegar helps to eliminate static cling (and it works effectively in my laundry fabric softener). With this in mind, and not wanting to give off a waft of vinegar as a perfume – I decided that instead I would use lemon juice to try as a quick fix.

You will need

200ml (7fl oz) spray bottle

1 tbsp lemon juice
150ml (5fl oz) water

Add the lemon juice and water to a spray bottle and shake to combine. I give a fine spray to my legs before putting on my trousers and I have to say I've had no problems. I have had followers test it for me too and the feedback was good.

Air-drying is less likely to cause static cling to clothing than a tumble dryer.

REMOVE BIRO, WAX CRAYON AND PAINT STAINS

Biro, whiteboard markers, paints, wax crayons and some inks on clothes and items that can go in the washing machine can be the most stubborn of stains and are best treated before washing. Once washed, the stains tend to become well and truly permanent, and while with a little time and perseverance they can fade, sometimes you are stuck with them forever. Treating them before washing is the best way.

Biro and paint on clothing, handbags, shoes, furniture and upholstery can be removed using surgical spirit very successfully. I have had followers who are delighted that biro has been removed from a whole range of non-clothing items made from leather, suede, corduroy and other materials.

You will need

a cotton pad (I use a cotton reusable make-up pad)
an upturned small bowl – for small items
an old towel for items of clothing

surgical spirit

For fixed non-washable items of furniture, handbags, shoes, upholstery, etc.

Dampen the cotton pad (using a small cotton pad is better than a big cloth because the whole pad can be soaked in the alcohol – a cleaning cloth absorbs too much). Using the pad, gently dab at the stain – no rubbing. A wet patch almost immediately evaporates along with the smell of the alcohol and, thankfully, the stain. Remember surgical spirit is flammable (as is any alcohol), so be sure there is no candle flickering alongside!

When removing a stain from leather or upholstery, gently dab at it until it fades and finally dissolves. Don't rub or scrub at the stain – take your time.

For clothing and washable items

When there is biro and paint on clothing I prefer to lay an old towel over an upturned bowl and place the biro/paint stain right side down onto the towel, then dab it again with the wetted cotton pad from the underside. The stain will transfer from the fabric onto the towel below rather than spread outwards onto the fabric.

When all else fails, some permanent markers, paints and inks are what they say and the only way I have found to remove them is to bleach them out of clothing.

You will need

small bowl or egg cup
a bowl
small spoon
artist's paintbrush

1 tsp green bleach
1–2 tbsp just-boiled water

Place the bleach granules into the egg cup, add the just-boiled water and stir until the granules dissolve, leaving a milky coloured, concentrated green bleach solution.

Lay the stained area over an upturned bowl, then dip the small paintbrush into the hot solution and paint over the permanent stain. Repeat at half-hour intervals until the ink stain has thoroughly faded and gone. This is only suitable for natural, white or light-coloured fabrics, though I have to say I managed to remove a long-standing brown stain from a lace jacket using this method. I didn't harm the lace or the colour.

Green bleach isn't brutal like chlorine and will slowly take its time to dissolve the stain, but remember it only remains active for a few hours so it isn't worth keeping the mix to use later – use what's left instead to clean the teapot and a few tea-stained cups, clean the sink, or pop into the washing machine with the whites load.

CLEAN MAKE-UP BRUSHES
AND SPONGES

I have a confession here. Even though I don't wear tonnes of make-up, my habit in the past – before I adopted my green credentials – was to throw away make-up brushes and sponges once they became really oily, hard or unsightly. I used disposable make-up pads and wipes too, happily tossing them into the bin on a daily basis. I never used to once think about the 'end of life' of these items or the unnecessary spend, and that ultimately they would all end up in landfill. Not one item that I was throwing away each day could ever be recycled.

With my green budget hat on I realized that sponges and brushes could easily be cleaned at home using products I already had – and being better cared for, they would last longer too. There were reusable make-up pads on the market and there was absolutely no need for me to be buying single-use cotton wool, wipes, make-up removers or brush-cleaning products.

You will need

    small pot
    metal sieve
    bowl of warm soapy water (I use eco-friendly washing-up
        liquid)

1 tbsp bicarbonate of soda

eco-friendly washing-up liquid (sufficient to make a thick
   paste)

500ml (17fl oz) tepid water mixed with 1 tbsp vinegar

After mixing together the bicarbonate of soda and the washing-up liquid to a paste in a small pot, dip in the brush or sponge that you want to clean so that it has a good covering, then use your hands to massage it in. I often use the palm of one hand as a bowl and massage the brush before rinsing and drying naturally.

Make-up and foundation is oily and greasy, but the paste will break this down. If the items are very soiled, give them a rinse in the bowl of warm soapy water then apply a further blob of paste. I then use the metal sieve, holding it in one hand while gently working the brushes against the wire with the other hand. The agitation allows the paste to get to the root of the bristles, releasing more make-up grease.

Once the brush is clean, give it a final rinse in tepid water with the vinegar added to dissolve any residual paste and soften the bristles. I wash sponges in the same way without the metal sieve, which would damage them.

Air-drying outside is the quickest method, and as with all brushes, lay them on their sides on a cloth so that moisture doesn't affect the glue holding the bristles in place or collect at the base of the brush, where it could go mouldy, or in the case of wooden brushes, start to rot.

How often should make-up brushes be cleaned? I think that has to be a personal decision. I don't wear a lot of make-up (and on gardening and cleaning days I don't wear any) and my brushes may be given a clean every couple of months or when they look grotty. Other people may wear make-up daily, in which case the cleaning regime needs to be stepped up accordingly.

RE-WAXING A JACKET

When I consider the clothes that I have bought then not worn, compared with the clothes that have become absolute favourites, have lasted years, and that I've loved and worn over and over, ashamedly the former far outweighs the latter!

I hope I am not the only one, but why is this? Is it because over the years I have been sucked into the latest fashion, this year's colour or seasonal must-have? The thought of the number of outfits I have bought for weddings, parties or a specific 'do' somewhere, never to be taken out of the wardrobe again, makes me shudder. I am trying to buy less now – not that I have ever been a huge follower of fashion – but it was evident from my packed wardrobe that I had much more than I needed. I wear the same collection of favourite clothes in rotation, so when I downsized my collection – the best of them going to the charity shop, the rest used for cleaning cloths, wet wipes or added to my gardening wardrobe – life then felt much easier. When I think about how many times I have tugged and pulled through the clothes in my packed wardrobe, frustrated in knowing that most of it I would never wear again, whereas now I've got just a few favourites hanging in plenty of space, it's easy to decide what to wear.

I have had a wax jacket for years – it used to be worn for best at the time when they were very much in fashion, then as time went on it became my dog-walking jacket. Warm, waterproof, sturdy and very much fit for purpose. However, one very wet and windy day it seemed to let me down. My shoulders felt damp and I don't think there is a worse feeling when out walking than when your legs, shoulders or feet are getting wet. It was all I could think about, these damp cold shoulders. Once home, it was off with the jacket (plus damp clothes underneath) and then when I inspected it I could see the lining inside was soaking wet all across the shoulder area. Water was coming in at the shoulder seams.

My initial thoughts were, 'Oh well, this jacket doesn't owe me anything, maybe I should buy a new one' – but a new one for dog walking!? They are so expensive to buy new. Then I had a look online and discovered they can be re-waxed, which was brilliant news – until I saw the price!

I had waterproofed boots before with this method, so decided to try it on my jacket. My jacket had mud splashes on the front, so I decided to give it a clean too.

You will need

TO CLEAN
large bowl
shower puff
old dry towel or cloth

2 tbsp washing soda
2 tbsp eco-friendly washing-up liquid
300ml (10fl oz) hot water

TO RE-WAX
spent candle (one that can be comfortably held – about the size of a bar of soap)
hairdryer

To clean

First, place the washing soda in the bowl, add the hot water and stir until dissolved, then add the washing-up liquid and use the shower puff to create lots of suds. The suds should reach the top of the bowl.

I prefer to do the next bit outside if weather permits. I spread the jacket out on my garden table, lining side down, then use the shower puff full of suds to work at the mud splashes and grubby parts of the jacket. As you clean each area, wipe it with the old dry towel to remove the loosened dirt and so that you are not soaking the jacket unnecessarily.

Once cleaned, hang the jacket outside to dry completely, or if there is no outside space or the weather isn't favourable, hang it inside in a warm, airy room.

To re-wax

I used an outside space to do the re-waxing, as I didn't want any wax pieces falling onto carpets or furnishings, but for those without an outside area I would cover a table or floor with newspapers or old packing paper or cardboard. I used my spent candle, started on the sleeves and rubbed it all over. Take time to concentrate on the garment's seams, especially on the shoulders, and any creases at the sleeves. When finished, the jacket should look as though it is covered in a thin layer of ice (that's the best way that I can describe it) with a thicker layer across all of the seams.

I then popped my jacket onto a coat hanger and took it into the garage (or find a suitable work space) and with hairdryer to hand started to complete the treatment. Immediately, as the hot air hits the jacket, the wax melts, the white frosty appearance disappears and the jacket looks shiny and new.

The wax doesn't drip off the coat, but soaks right into the fabric.

Test time. The first time I did this treatment I then took a watering can with a rose attached and poured a heavy shower of water over my coat. I was absolutely delighted that the water just ran off it – my shoulder seams and the whole coat were once again waterproof, well cleaned and maybe looking too good to wear as my dog-walking coat!

BEESWAX BREAD BAG

If your home-made bread is popped into a plastic bag, mould will quickly form because the bread's moisture as it evaporates will have nowhere to go. There are breathable bread bags on the market – often still made from plastic but with tiny per-forations to allow some airflow to the bread inside. As well as the expense incurred, and the fact that the bags are plastic (and we are trying to turn our backs on plastic), the ones I have tried have not been too robust and have split at the seams after a couple of uses.

When I was a child there was always a bread bin in the kitchen and a bought loaf used to be sold in waxed paper. So I thought a good idea would be to make a reusable, washable, long-lasting cotton bag, coated in beeswax, which would remain breathable and, thanks to the anti-bacterial qualities of beeswax, would resist mould too. A great gift idea.

I have made beeswax wraps in the past and always used the oven for melting the wax. This time, due to the piece of fabric being larger than any of my oven trays, the extra expense of switching on the oven, and for speed, I decided to use my iron. Much cheaper, much easier, no mess and no washing up.

You will need

very thin cotton fabric, I used white muslin (whatever size
    suits you, mine measured 30cm x 80cm (12in x 31in))
pinking shears (to prevent fraying) or scissors
large old clean bath towel

2 sheets greaseproof paper larger than the piece of fabric
up to 100g (3½oz) beeswax pellets
iron
sewing machine or needle and thread

Cut the piece of fabric to the size you want, and make sure it has no creases (iron it first if it has).

Lay out the towel on a work surface and cover with a sheet of greaseproof paper larger than the fabric to be used for the bag. Lay the fabric over the paper in a single layer without any folds or creases. Scatter over an even layer of beeswax pellets – not too many, as you can go back and fill in any gaps later. Imagine that each pellet will melt to double its size, so space them accordingly. It is worth taking your time here to ensure even distribution. Cover with the second sheet of greaseproof paper so that all of the fabric and all of the pellets are covered.

Switch on the 'dry' iron – do not select steam – and choose a medium heat. Place the iron onto the paper and slowly work over the fabric, and you will see that the beeswax readily melts underneath. It is possible to identify through the translucent paper any areas where the beeswax hasn't quite covered, so you can peel back the paper and slot a few extra pellets in here and there if needed, then replace the paper and iron over.

Once you can see that the whole piece of fabric is darkened by melted wax, peel back the top sheet of paper while still hot, quickly followed by the bottom sheet. The waxed fabric will almost immediately cool and stiffen.

Lay the waxed fabric in one piece on a work surface and decide where the bottom of the bag will be. You will need to allow for a flap at the top end which will fold over to seal the bag. The bottom crease therefore needs to be made 7.5 or 10cm (3 or 4 inches) below the halfway point. Press down with your hand; if the sides are not quite square after folding you may want to tidy them up using pinking shears.

Now that the fabric is completely cold and stiffened, has a neat crease at the base and neat sides, either hand-sew the sides (wrong sides) together to make the bag or use a sewing machine.

The bread bag can be washed in warm soapy water and air-dried as necessary. After many uses and folds the wax will leave crease marks, but just like beeswax wraps the whole item can be easily refreshed. Slot a piece of kitchen foil or a new piece of greaseproof paper inside (so that the bag sides don't stick together), then place two pieces of greaseproof paper once more on the top and bottom, rest on a towel and iron the bag again. No extra beeswax is needed, because as the wax melts again, the creases are covered and the bag is as good as the day it was made.

DARNING

Everyone used to darn socks, and I understand why – they probably had knitted them in the first place and knew how much time and effort had gone into their making. Nowadays a pack of machine-made socks, containing probably three or five pairs, can be so cheap that repairing them is not worth the while. Equally, the socks are of such poor quality that after a few wears they break a hole at the toe, but that's fine – we throw them away and buy another pack.

For me this behaviour is now a thing of the past. I pay for one pair of socks probably what I used to pay for five – quality, not quantity. This is also reflected in their comfort, durability, thickness, and also they become my favourites! I cherish my quality socks and when one sprang a hole at the toe I decided to darn it – something I had not done for many decades, but I have to say I enjoyed it. Darning and visible mending and patching is becoming very popular and some of it looks amazing.

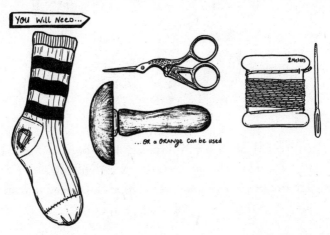

YOU WILL NEED...

...OR a ORANGE can be used

2Meters

You will need

darning mushroom or an orange
darning needle (see below)
embroidery thread in your chosen colours

To darn a simple sock hole you will need either a darning mushroom (a wooden tool that looks like a mushroom, with the stalk used as a handle and the dome of the mushroom used to open out the hole). If you don't have the tool, use a small orange. Push the darning tool into the site of the hole – very often the foot of the sock. This will open up and expose the hole. Don't be tempted to sew the hole together, as the sock will probably burst open again later because it will have been reduced in size.

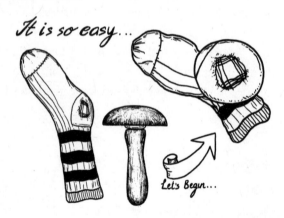

It is so easy...

Let's Begin...

For thread, I often use embroidery silks because there are so many colours to choose from that there will always be one to match the repair – although the colours don't need to match, of course. I darned a pair of long purple winter socks with white snowflakes on the legs. When I darned the toe, I added a white snowflake at the toe rather than darn in purple – personalized socks! Embroidery silks are designed to be split into strands, so I use one of the six strands, threaded through a darning needle (a needle with a large eye and blunted point) and continue as follows.

With the hole facing you, run a long first thread from right to left across the hole, secure with a stitch at the left of the hole, then run it back, left to right. Continue until the hole has been covered with a grid of horizontal threads close together – they are not pulled tight but instead have infilled that worn hole in the sock.

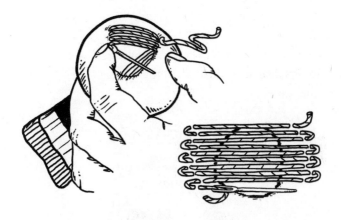

Complete the darn by running the thread from top to bottom, only this time the needle and thread will be woven over and under the horizontal threads already made. I enjoy this part. Weave close together under and over from bottom to top. The second row from top to bottom will take on the opposite weave, i.e. if the previous thread went over, this one will go under, so that what you will have created is a neat carpet of thread that completely repairs the hole, making it thick and strong yet beautiful.

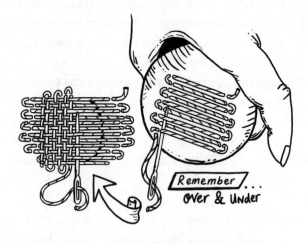

My grandmother used to keep her darning box in the lounge ready to repair socks and gloves in the evenings – I have started to do the same!

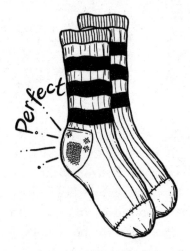

TEDDY AND SOFT TOY MAKEOVER

If you, your children or any family members have a favourite soft toy – teddy, rabbit, elephant, you name it – chances are it is well loved, and because it is well loved it has probably been well handled, has sat alongside an ill child, has travelled far and wide, and as a result may be a bit smelly and a bit grubby.

I have Tid; he's not a childhood bear but I have certainly had him for several decades. He hadn't suffered much wear and tear because all he did was sit on my bed, until one day Wilfred (dog) came across him, befriended him and took him out to play.

Thankfully the weather was dry, but even so he was certainly looking the worse for wear. His jumper was grubby and his fur was dirty too. Upon inspection, there was a label that stated he should not be washed and I know from experience that washing a soft toy can sometimes dislodge the stuffing inside, making it lumpy, misshapen and certainly looking out of sorts. Here's what to do.

You will need

clean towel
small bowl
small towel or flannel
small soft clothes, hair or sink brush
bowl of tepid clean water
50ml (1¾fl oz) liquid detergent (see page 52)
2 tbsp bicarbonate of soda
1 tsp eco-friendly washing-up liquid

To clean toy clothes

If the cuddly toy has any clothing at all, remove and wash that first. The clothing Tid had was simply a little hand-knitted jumper, so I decided to clean this by soaking it in a small bowl of tepid water with 50ml (1¾fl oz) home-made detergent. I left it for several hours, but overnight would be fine. Following the long soak, give it a gentle rinse in tepid water and lay it flat on a clean towel to dry. I would suggest a non-agitated tepid wash for any toy clothing to avoid shrinkage, especially on old, much-loved items.

To clean the teddy

Measure the bicarbonate of soda into a small bowl, add the washing-up liquid then sufficient tepid water to make a thin paste about the consistency of single cream. Use your hands to massage the paste into all of the fur, paying particular attention to the grubby areas. Once the bear or soft toy is covered in paste, leave it for 10–15 minutes.

Fill a bowl with tepid clean water, dampen and wring-out a small towel or flannel and begin to work at removing the paste, while at the same time working at the fur, massaging it this way and that. Rinse the cloth regularly and notice how grubby the water becomes!

Take time rinsing, wringing and wiping until you reveal a clean teddy or soft toy, though his fur may look clumped. You haven't saturated him with water so there's no chance of him shrinking. If he was a bit smelly the bicarbonate of soda will neutralize the odour too.

Leave to dry outside if the weather is fine, and away from direct heat if inside. Once completely dry use a soft clothes brush, soft clean hair brush or clean sink brush and work at the fur to loosen it and brush away residual bicarb. This is much better done outside.

The fur will be fluffed up, clean and sweet smelling now, so it's back on with the clean clothes and back onto the bed.

REUSABLE WET WIPES

Small plastic packets of wet wipes are very handy and over the years I have been one of the many individuals who didn't really think about their effect on the environment or the recurrent cost, because so often I used to open a pack, use one or two, and then not reseal the pack sufficiently and the contents would dry out, be thrown away and a new pack bought – and so on. The single-use plastic packets go into landfill, to take many decades to decompose, while the wipes themselves can end up in all kinds of places – some down the toilet, to end up making a contribution to huge fatbergs in our drainage systems, others that are discarded after picnics or a day out at the beach may be blown around to end up in our rivers and oceans.

Since going green, single-use wipes of any kind (make-up, cleaning, polishing, etc.) were one of my first swaps, and I now dislike them with a vengeance. Unfortunately, they are on sale everywhere and I fully understand why people buy them – they can get you out of a sticky situation, especially if there is nowhere available to wash or clean up messy hands.

I believe there are now biodegradable wipes hitting the market, but again there is the 'single-use' element, plus the expense. In addition, I have read worrying articles about misleading terms when it comes to 'biodegradable'. When we think about it, everything is biodegradable – even a plastic bottle – it is just how long it takes to biodegrade that is relevant. A plastic bottle can take 350 years. The buzz word we need to be looking for is 'compostable', to know that what we are buying is truly eco-friendly. Rather than doing that, we can make our own reusable wipes without any damage to the environment and for a fraction of the cost, and when they are finally past their best they are compostable.

I came up with this little idea after finding myself needing to eat a sandwich while travelling on a train. There was nowhere to wash my hands, the train was busy and I knew I had touched all kinds of surfaces. I had been on escalators, needed to visit not the cleanest public toilet, and as a result my hands felt very grubby and unhygienic. Needless to say, I wanted to resist my sandwich but had to give in and cover my hand with the wrapper to eat it the best way I could.

These wipes are a super simple upcycle for old clothes too – cut-up cotton t-shirts are perfect for these, as there's no machine edging necessary because it doesn't fray, and the fabric can be slightly stretchy too, so it's great for wiping hands.

MAKES 20 WIPES

You will need

20 x 15–20cm (6–8in) squares of thin cotton fabric scraps
bowl
20ml (¾fl oz) aloe vera gel (mild cleanser and skin
 moisturizer)
small whisk
120ml (4fl oz) water
30ml (1fl oz) surgical spirit (anti-bac cleanser)
2–3 drops organic lemon essential oil for fragrance
 (optional)

small plastic box with airtight lid (handy size to keep in the
    car or handbag)
small plastic bag
permanent pen or label to mark the box
funnel
small plastic or glass 500ml (17fl oz) bottle or jar with lid

After cutting the fabric squares, wet them thoroughly with cold water and wring them out so that not a single drop of water can be squeezed further. In the bowl, add the aloe vera gel and beat with the small whisk with a few tablespoons of the water to emulsify and take it from a thick gel to a runny solution. Add the rest of the water followed by the surgical spirit, then the organic essential oil, if using. The solution will turn milky white.

———

NOTE: If you want to make an alcohol-free
wipe (without the anti-bacterial qualities),
leave out the surgical spirit.

———

Drop the dampened fabric squares into the solution, ensuring they absorb the liquid, then wring them out. Fold each one separately and lay it into the plastic box. Cover with a folded plastic bag so that you have somewhere to put the soiled wipes to bring home. The residual liquid can be used for the next batch of wipes; simply use the funnel to decant into a small bottle and keep it on the shelf for later.

Label the box and keep it in the car or in your bag. I had a number of questions about whether the cloths start to smell, go mouldy or dry out. I kept a box for two months – no mould, no unpleasant smell, and in an airtight plastic box they didn't dry out.

To launder the wipes, I treat them as I do my reusable make-up pads (see page 73), though you may prefer to wash them all together in a small zip-up laundry bag so that they don't get mixed up with the rest of the laundry.

DE-ICER

Frozen windscreens in the wintertime used to call for one of two habits. My first used to be to go outside, switch on the engine, put the screen heater on and just leave the car polluting the atmosphere while idling away and melting the ice in its own time. My second was to buy an aerosol can, spray it all over with various chemicals, and watch the ice melt quickly while I did my bit to destroy the ozone layer. Aerosol cans are not easy to dispose of responsibly either.

There are ice scrapers, of course, which are effective and some may prefer those, but when I realized I had a stash of plastic spray bottles I decided to work on a little recipe. It's a simple little gift idea too – I even included a small one in my Christmas hampers!

You will need

200ml (7fl oz) spray bottle
digital weighing scales
funnel

120ml (4fl oz) surgical spirit
25ml (1fl oz) water
2–3 drops eco-friendly washing-up liquid

Easy to mix straight into the bottle. Stand the bottle onto the scales with the funnel in the neck and cancel the weight to zero. First add the surgical spirit, set the scale to zero again, then add the water and lastly the eco-friendly washing-up liquid, which will help to emulsify the two. Give it a shake and it is ready to go.

The first time I used this spray it melted the ice on the windscreen quickly at the outset and I was off in my car without harmful 'idling'. That same day the temperature didn't go above freezing. I returned to my car six hours later and the untreated section of the windscreen was frozen yet my sprayed area was still clear.

SCREEN WASH

I have often wondered why proprietary screen wash needs to be coloured blue. I hadn't thought about whether it was having a negative impact on the environment when I began researching a cheaper alternative to the large plastic containers of the liquid.

I then decided one rainy afternoon to do some reading around 'screen wash' and spent a worrying time going through the eighteen-page hazard data sheet of a well-known brand. I was saddened by the number of harmful chemicals involved and thought about how many times I had readily squirted my screen, let the car use its wipers to clean the screen and toss the excess toxic waste onto the road, down the drains and into our waterways.

I knew distilled water was better than tap water for screen wash as there are no mineral deposits that may clog up car pipes and nozzles, and then turned my attention to what Mother Nature has on offer for free – rainwater!

Just by sheer coincidence, I came across an article that suggested a car manufacturer may be looking into the possibility of being able to capture the rainwater that falls on the car and then drain and filter this into the screen-wash bottle under the bonnet. What a fantastic thought, but until that is happening to my car, I will continue with this simple recipe.

You will need

2 litre (4 pint) plastic bottle
digital weighing scales

funnel
fine-mesh tea strainer

1.5 litres (50fl oz) clean rainwater
125ml (4½fl oz) surgical spirit
3ml eco-friendly washing-up liquid

Capture clean rainwater from a water butt or even from under the down pipe when the rain is falling fast – you'll be surprised how clean and clear it is.

I mix the screen wash directly in the bottle. Place the empty bottle onto the scales with the funnel in the neck and zero the weight.

Filter the rainwater through the tea strainer, straight into the bottle. The tea strainer will capture any debris. Zero the scales again and add the surgical spirit, which will not only keep the water clean and prevent it turning green, it will also clean the screen quicker than using water on its own. An added benefit is that it will also prevent freezing up to -5°C (23°F).

Finally, add a little washing-up liquid – only a few drops – which will help to dissolve greasy deposits on the windscreen. Shake the bottle and the mix is made. Label the bottle – I keep mine in the garage and top up the screen-wash bottle when required.

For those with more severe winters, this may be suitable only as a summer screen wash.

WORKING HANDS AND SORE
CRACKED FEET CREAM

Gardening, housework, working outdoors and unfortunately the ageing process all take their toll on hands and feet. I used to spend that bit more money on a good tube or tub of effective hand cream. Those tubes that contain a runny though very perfumed cream are no good to me; I need a thick, wholesome cream that I can feel soothe and smooth out my dry working hands and heels.

Once, when I came to the end of my expensive tub of cream, I decided to research the ingredients. Again, the chemicals and undecipherable contents numbered around sixteen – the one that I did recognize was petroleum. So after examining my own shelf of natural ingredients I decided to make my own for less money and with fewer ingredients, and the resulting cream is so good, plus a little goes a very long way. Save your cream pots and add this to your collection of home-made favourites.

MAKES 300ML (10FL OZ) – I FILLED
3 LARGE AND 2 SMALL CREAM POTS

You will need

digital weighing scales
heatproof mixing bowl
small saucepan
plastic spatula

stick blender or electric hand whisk

reusable piping bag

pint glass

clean pots with lids

120g (4¼oz) coconut oil

60g (2¼oz) beeswax pellets (I used white ones, which gave me a gorgeous finished cream)

300ml (10fl oz) water

50ml (2fl oz) oil (vegetable, sunflower, olive oil or oil of choice)

40ml (1¼fl oz) vegetable glycerine

4–5 drops essential oil for perfume (optional)

Begin by weighing the coconut oil and beeswax pellets into the mixing bowl. Heat the water in the saucepan until boiling, then turn down to a simmer. Stand the mixing bowl on top and stir with a spatula until the coconut oil and pellets dissolve together. The coconut oil will melt first and quickly, whereas the pellets will take 5 minutes or so.

Once all the solids are melted, take the bowl off the heat, put the saucepan to one side, but don't discard the hot water.

Place the bowl onto a work surface then add the oil and, using the stick blender or electric hand whisk, mix and emulsify. Then add the vegetable glycerine and essential oil, if using.

Continue to whisk or blitz until the cream begins to thicken and cool slightly. Use the previously boiled water from the pan to then add hot water, 1 tablespoon at a time, blitzing well between each addition. The ideal consistency should be that of thick, whipped-up double cream.

I found it easier to dispense the cream neatly into the pots using a reusable piping bag without a nozzle fitted. Fold the wide end of the piping bag over the rim of the pint glass, then you have both hands free to pour the warm cream into the neck without spilling. Pipe the warm cream into the pots, leave to cool and firm up, then screw the tops on.

This hand cream has a shelf life of at least a year – probably in line with proprietary products. I was still using mine long after the 12 months.

TIP: If you are looking for a cheap, effective, eco-friendly hand cleaner, try my cream cleaner (see page 14). Apart from its many other uses, I have found it cleans up the dirtiest of hands, including oil and paint, and as it contains vegetable glycerine it is kind and doesn't dry the skin.

CLEVER KITCHEN

M any people have their own 'cleverness' in the kitchen, and I have included this chapter to share some of my favourites. Whether it be a microwave quickie to save on energy, a tip that you never thought could be that good, or simply ideas that make better use of your appliances and save you money.

I have included a number of my favourite recipes, too – my best, of course, being the low-cost or 'free' food wonders, those that avoid food waste and those that use little or no energy to make. A number of flexi-recipes here can be adapted and made using the appliances you already have, and I hope they will help in your endeavours to save money, save energy and our planet. I will show you how, with a little attention to detail, the cheapest of recipes can produce baked treats that look as though they have come not from your clever kitchen but from the display window of the best patisserie in France.

FRIENDLY FREEZER

For the budget-conscious, eco-friendly, no-food-waste-minded of us, the modern household freezer is an absolute gem. Efficient to run, when used well it means we can hang on to our home-grown produce, buy in bulk and save some money, as well as avoid food waste and have a handy meal to cook from frozen when we are in a rush. Many foods freeze very well, some need special attention, and others do not freeze well and are not worth the effort. There are a few simple rules to successful freezing which I will try to explain succinctly.

Open-freezing

Home-grown soft berries, foraged blackberries and seasonal soft fruits bought for a song at the market (apart from straw-berries) can be frozen as they are without any freezer prep at all – as can sliced peppers, leeks, apples and pears.

If, however, you pop them into bags or boxes as they are, when you come to use them, they will probably have frozen into a solid lump due to their high water content. To avoid this and ensure your foods are separate and free-flowing once frozen, it is necessary to 'open-freeze' them first. Simply lay the berries, apple pieces (tossed in sugar first to prevent browning), pepper slices, sliced leeks or pears in a single layer on a tray and pop into the freezer for about an hour. When you take them from the freezer they will be firm and can then be transferred to freezer bags or boxes. Soft fruits I freeze for a year.

Freezing Other Foods

Foods that freeze well are pies, cakes, bread, blanched vegetables, eggs, milk, cheese, whole chillies, root ginger, lemongrass, garlic, pizza, meringues, stews, soups, casseroles, buttercream and eggs.

EGG WHITES: I freeze each egg white in a silicone teacake mould then, once frozen, I have a handy dome shape that I pop into a bag with the rest. When I need three egg whites for a recipe (meringues, macarons, buttercreams or angel cakes, for example), I can grab myself three handy frozen domes, then pop them into a clean bowl where they will thaw at room temperature in an hour or two. Egg whites I freeze for up to 6 months.

EGG YOLKS: Freeze in small plastic pots with a well-fitting lid, mark on the lid the number of yolks being frozen. I sprinkle over a scattering of either sugar or salt depending whether I am more likely to use them in a sweet or savoury dish. The sugar/salt will prevent the yolk's skin from developing a thick, rubbery texture. Egg yolks I freeze for up to 3 months.

FOODS THAT DON'T FREEZE WELL: Custard turns grainy in texture. Jelly – the gelatine will deteriorate and jelly will no longer be jelly. Tomatoes will lose their structure, so they're perfect for cooking with later but not to eat fresh; however, it can be a quick way to remove the skins – once frozen, the tomato skins just peel off. Double cream freezes better than single cream but, even then, I think the taste and texture changes and is not pleasant. Use surplus cream to make butter instead (see page 211). Yoghurt goes grainy; better to bake into a cake then freeze. Cream cheese loses texture and turns grainy.

Avoid Freezer Burn

If you have heard of freezer burn it may sound like a contradiction. How can something burn in a freezer? You will know when you see it. I bought fresh fish one time and decided to open-freeze the fillets as described above so that they could then be packed singly into one bag and I could easily take out just one or maybe two fillets and not a solid frozen lump of six fillets that would have to all be thawed at once. My fish was duly laid out on paper on a tray and popped into the freezer for half an hour to firm up.

Trouble was, I forgot about the fish completely until I visited the freezer maybe three or four days later. The fish had, of course, frozen solid, but rather than being still white and fresh, having only been openly exposed long enough to just firm up, it was dry looking, darker in colour and 'burnt' by the freezer. Very disappointing, because we know how expensive fresh fish is. I didn't waste it – it wasn't inedible, but it was hard and discoloured once thawed. I used it to make fish pies. I now put the timer on when I open-freeze.

Freezer burn, therefore, is the result of inadequate wrapping and when food has been frozen for way too long. It is important that home-frozen food is wrapped adequately to avoid freezer burn and what I call freezer odour. Freezer bags and boxes are 'fit for purpose' and plastic freezer bags are very thick for this very reason. Reusable freezer boxes, too, are robust, ensuring the foods will not deteriorate quickly. If you have ever wrapped some foods for the freezer simply in cling film, thin plastic or a loose wrap of foil, it may be that once thawed after a long time the food has dried, discoloured or has a freezer 'smell' to it.

Labelling

How many times have you popped something into the freezer, convinced you will remember what it is, to then at some later date, months later, realize you have absolutely no idea what it is supposed to be, how long it has been there and, consequently, are too worried to take the chance of eating it. So it ends up in the bin. Labelling and dating can seem tedious at the time but, trust me, it is very helpful and avoids disappointing mistakes.

I once took out a tub of what I was convinced was a vegetable chilli from the freezer in the morning, popped it into the fridge and looked forward to enjoying a quick meal when I came in at the end of the day. To my huge disappointment when I returned home – cold, tired and hungry – and lifted the lid from the container, which had now thoroughly thawed, what was staring back at me was a tub of chocolate buttercream. Delicious, but now was not the time or the place!

FRESH GINGER SUPER SAVER

Ever bought a root of fresh ginger, used a thumb-sized piece, popped it back into the pack and then into the fridge? The next time you need fresh ginger you know you have some, but when revisited it has shrivelled up, dried out, softened and at worst turned mouldy. Only good for the compost bin. I buy a large root of fresh ginger about twice a year. Once home I wash and dry it, break it into a few pieces, pop them into a bag or box and freeze until required. When a recipe calls for fresh ginger I take out a piece, grate it from frozen (skin and all) then pop it back into the freezer. The same applies to lemongrass and fresh chillies, both of which I freeze whole.

GORGEOUS GARLIC PEELING
AND PREP TRICK

I came across a half-price bag of bargain garlic and came home with about ten large juicy bulbs. Rather than risk it starting to sprout, go soft or mouldy before I had the chance to use it, I decided to freeze it. The tedious part for me is peeling the individual cloves, though this can be sped up. All you need are two same-sized, large metal bowls or a metal bowl with a metal plate to cover.

Push on the garlic bulb with the palm of your hand to break out the cloves, then separate and place the papery skin-covered cloves into the metal bowl.

Position the second bowl or metal plate over the top, hold securely with both hands, then shake vigorously, banging the cloves repeatedly up and down against the metal sides and top. Give yourself a decent workout, banging and shaking for about a minute.

Just like a potato 'rumbler peeler', the skins will leave the fleshy cloves inside the bowl. Even if at first it appears the skins are still intact, you will realize they are loose and will either fall off or easily peel away, leaving creamy white, undamaged, peeled garlic cloves.

Just as onion skins are edible and nutritious, garlic skins are too (rich in vitamins A, C and E and numerous antioxidants), so rather than tossing them into the compost, blitz them to a powder to make a mild garlic seasoning – great to sprinkle onto roast potatoes, add into stews or to any recipe that calls for garlic.

The gorgeous peeled cloves can then be popped into a box and into the freezer. When needed, take a clove – it is not too hard or brittle and can easily be chopped, sliced or grated in its frozen state and used straight away.

I have kept garlic in the freezer for up to six months or until I have used it up. Alternatively, freeze whole garlic bulbs and use as required, though I do like to be able to quickly retrieve a few pre-prepped cloves from the freezer when I am rushing to get the tea on!

KNOW YOUR ONIONS

I understand this is not really a budgeting tip and may not be news to many readers, but once I learned to chop an onion finely my life was changed. For years my onion chopping was very erratic. Any recipe that called for a finely chopped onion would actually include large chunks that had slipped away under the knife and small shards that had also escaped, along with a selection of smallish dice. The result was that some pieces fried very quickly, the shards stuck blackened to the base of the pan and the larger pieces sometimes didn't soften at all and created a bitterness to my soups and stews. If this is you, then read on. Take the onion and slice off the top (the leaf end). At the root end slice just enough to clean up any of the rough stubbly root. Don't cut the root off. Peel the onion of the layers of papery skin until you have a whole white onion. With a sharp knife then slice the onion in half lengthways from the leaf end down to the root.

Hold the onion cut side down on a smooth surface with one hand and gently slide the knife across it, halting at the root and not cutting all the way through. If the onion is large, make a second cut above the first one, again stopping before the root. The chunky root end I add to my bag of vegetable stock scraps.

The onion skins can be added to the compost, to the bag of vegetable scraps to be used later in stocks.

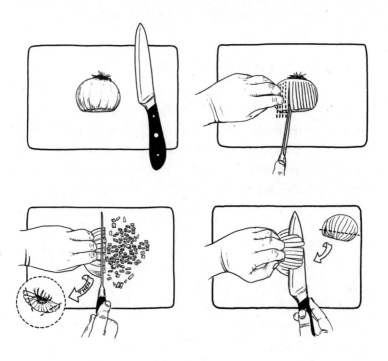

TIP: Wash and air-dry onion skins – use a dehydrator if you have one, but I find they dry very quickly on a dry cloth in a warm room. Once completely crisp they can be quickly blitzed to a crumb or powder, transferred to a recycled spice or herb jar and stored indefinitely. Free food!

DON'T FORGET THE WASHING-UP!

I realize there will be readers living already in super-efficient households with 'on tap' hot water. For me, though, the hot water takes forever to come through and as well as the waste of cold water having to run down the sink before I can enjoy hot for washing up, I now consider the time, effort, waste and expense for just one bowl of water.

For Aga owners
My hot water takes such a long time to come through the pipes that I now keep a large pan or casserole with a lid in the bottom oven for a regular supply of hot water with no waste and no extra cost.

For those with a wood-burning stove
Invest in a small stove kettle, filled and ready to boil up on top of the stove during the winter months for tea, coffee or washing up.

Electric oven
If the oven is on for something else and there is free space, pop in a lidded casserole or covered bowl of water to give sufficient for washing up after the meal. Even a bowl or large jug filled with water popped into the oven after cooking will often heat sufficiently for washing up using up residual free heat from the turned-off oven.

Kettle

I enjoy a cuppa after a meal and if the kettle is therefore going on anyway and there are maybe not many pots to wash, I will fill the kettle, let it get hot, switch off and pour more than half into the washing-up bowl. Back on with the kettle to boil the remaining water for my cuppa. On these occasions, rather than draining off what seems like gallons from my hot water tank, I boil just what I need in the kettle. I am certainly saving water and probably significant energy too. Just a reminder to descale your kettle regularly – limescale is not only corrosive but will make your kettle inefficient, needing more energy and time to reach a boil.

MAKE YOUR OWN PAPER CUPCAKE CASES, PLUS PENNY-WISE RECIPES

Ever decided to bake a few small cakes or muffins only to find you are completely out of paper cupcake cases? These handy cases are much cheaper than the plastic-packaged, factory-produced alternatives and I think are more rustic and attractive, too.

MAKES 12

You will need

greaseproof or baking paper
scissors
a drinking glass with a base that fits perfectly into the base
of your 12-hole deep muffin tin

We will make twelve 9cm (3.5in) squares from the greaseproof or baking paper. As the rolls of paper generally are 37cm (14.5 in) wide, make two concertina folds in the lengths of paper at 9cm (3.5in) intervals, then cut along the length. Cut each length into three, then fold each of these in half and then in half again and cut into neat 9cm (3.5in) squares.

Take each square separately, turn the glass upside down and centre the paper over the base. Using your palms, mould the paper over the base. Repeat the moulding over and over using first one hand, then the other until the paper forms the shape of the glass. Lift off the paper case and pop into the base of

the cupcake tin. Repeat until all twelve cups are filled then use in any of the following recipes.

Raspberry and Almond Muffins

I couldn't help but do a quick cost comparison, and a home-made muffin can be around a quarter of the price of a bought one. Obviously, there is the energy cost involved, but baking now only happens at a time when I am putting the oven on for something else. These simple cake batters will sit in the fridge for up to four hours in the bowl, to be transferred to the baking cases when the oven is up and running.

I love using frozen raspberries in cakes, though if they are popped into the batter whole the weight of them can cause them to sink, and because they are frozen the cake batter around them will not cook and will be soggy and unpleasant. To avoid this, place the measure of frozen raspberries into a plastic bag and crush them with a rolling pin. The resultant frozen raspberry crumbs will bake evenly without affecting the consistency of the sponge.

MAKES 12

You will need

medium mixing bowl
hand-held electric whisk
spatula
ice cream scoop or tablespoon
paper cases

130g (4¼oz) softened butter or margarine
125g (4¼oz) caster or granulated sugar
2 eggs
30g (1oz) ground almonds (or use ground rice for a tenth of the price, see page 262)
130g (4¼oz) self-raising flour
1 tsp almond extract
100g (3½oz) frozen, crushed raspberries
1 tbsp flaked almonds to scatter a few over each cake
icing sugar, for dusting (optional)

Place the butter or margarine, sugar, eggs, ground almonds or ground rice, flour and almond extract into a bowl and whisk with the hand-held electric whisk until the batter is well mixed and smooth. Add the frozen raspberry crumbs and fold these through briefly with a spatula (just three to four stirs) – not too much or the batter will turn pink as the juice from the frozen crumbs begins to thaw.

Use the ice cream scoop or spoon to divide the batter between the 12 cases, scatter over a few flaked almonds, then bake for 20–25 minutes at 180°C/160°C fan/350°F/gas 4, or until risen and golden. Leave to cool in the tins then lift out and dust with icing sugar, if desired. If the oven is on anyway pop these cakes in, otherwise the batter can sit in the fridge until ready to bake.

Chocolate Chip Muffins

MAKES 12

Replace the ground almonds with 30g (1oz) cocoa powder and 50ml (1¾fl oz) milk

Replace 1 tsp almond extract with 1 tsp vanilla extract

Replace the crushed raspberries with 50g (1¾oz) chocolate chips

This is simply a variation on Raspberry and Almond Muffins using the same ingredients but with a few substitutions as listed above. Follow the method, but replace the ground almonds with cocoa powder and milk, and the almond extract with vanilla extract. Then stir through chocolate chips rather than crushed raspberries at the end and omit the flaked almonds.

Crunchy Lemon Drizzle Muffins

MAKES 12

Remove the ground almonds and ground rice and increase
  self-raising flour to 150g (5½oz)
Add the finely grated zest and juice of 1 lemon
Replace 1 tsp almond extract with 1 tsp lemon extract
50g (1¾oz) granulated sugar

Another variation of my muffin sponge recipe with a few
citrussy swaps.

Follow the method as for the Raspberry and Almond
Muffins, replacing the ground almonds with extra flour, and
the almond extract with lemon extract. Add to the sponge mix
the lemon zest and half of the juice and transfer to the paper
cupcake cases in the tin.

Mix the juice of the other half of the lemon with the sugar
and brush this over the hot cakes as soon as they come out
of the oven, while they are still in the tins. Once cool and dry
this glaze will give a crunchy, zingy lemon topping.

STRAWBERRY-TOP VINEGAR

When the strawberry season is upon us we know that summer has arrived, and nothing beats the taste of the freshest, bright red berries. Whether you grow your own, buy them almost daily because they are cheap, or have been out to pick your own for jamming, don't let the tops go to waste.

MAKES 500ML (17FL OZ)

You will need

knife
large glass jar with a lid, sufficient to hold 500ml (17fl oz)
   liquid plus strawberry tops
strainer
jug
attractive 500ml (17fl oz) vinegar bottle
funnel
paper coffee filter or square of kitchen paper

sliced green tops from a punnet of strawberries (about
   20-30 tops of different sizes)
500ml (17fl oz) distilled white vinegar

After washing your strawberries, rather than hull them, slice off the very tops of the leaves with a tiny section of the fruit. Pop the tops into a jar. Once all of the strawberries have been trimmed and transferred to the jar, pour over the vinegar, screw on the lid and leave in a cool place (not the fridge) for 2–3 days.

After the standing time the vinegar will be tinged with a gorgeous strawberry colour and a fruity smell. Strain the vinegar from the tops using the strainer set over a jug.

Take your clean vinegar bottle, pop the funnel into the neck and line it with either the paper coffee filter or fold a sheet of absorbent kitchen paper into four and open it out into a cone. Then pour the strained vinegar through the filter and allow it to drip down into the bottle.

You will have 500ml (17fl oz) strawberry-top vinegar to be used in any recipe that calls for cider vinegar, white wine vinegar or red wine vinegar. Keeps for up to two months.

Simple Strawberry Vinaigrette

MAKES SUFFICIENT DRESSING FOR ONE SIDE DISH

You will need

jam jar with screw top, or similar

75ml (2½fl oz) strawberry-top vinegar
90ml (3fl oz) olive oil
1 tsp mustard powder
salt and pepper, to taste

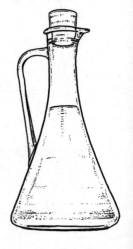

Measure all the ingredients into a clean glass jar with a screw top, give it a shake, and it is ready to use as a salad dressing or to pour over cooked or raw vegetables. It will keep in the fridge for 3–4 days.

BUDGET BAKED POTATO!

When I saw that supermarkets were selling crispy skinned, oven-baked jacket potatoes topped with a drizzle of oil and ready to pop into the microwave, for a ridiculous price, I was inspired to come up with my own version. With energy prices where they are now, it doesn't feel right to put the oven on for just two or three potatoes. I realize a potato can be baked in the microwave, but I am a fan of a crispy skin rather than the steamed version that the microwave produces. A smarter way, however, is to make the very best use of the energy, and instead of baking two or three potatoes at a time, I bake 20!

You will need

fork
teaspoon
large mixing bowl
potato masher or ricer
tray for open freezing
freezer bags or boxes

20 large baking potatoes (roughly 200g/7oz each)
oil, for rubbing
250g (9oz) butter
a slosh of milk or cream
salt and pepper, to taste

300g (10½oz) grated cheese
any leftover chopped cooked ham, bacon or mushrooms
chopped chives, spring onions, fresh chilli

Wash the potatoes and leave them to drain and dry. Prick each one with a fork several times to prevent the skins from splitting, then rub a drop of oil between your hands and use it to coat each potato to ensure they bake with a crispy skin. Preheat the oven to 200°C/180°C fan/400°F/gas 6.

Carefully space the potatoes evenly on two shelves in the hot oven and bake for 1–1½ hours depending on the size of the potatoes – until the skins are crisp and the potatoes feel soft when squeezed. Remove them from the oven and leave until cool enough to handle.

Cut each potato in half lengthways and use the teaspoon to scoop out the soft potato and drop into the bowl. Lay the empty potato halves on a tray, cut side uppermost. Mash the soft potato with room-temperature butter and milk, salt and pepper until soft and creamy, then fold in additional fillings of choice – cheese, cooked bacon, ham, spring onions, etc. Mix all together well then spoon the filling into the cooked potato jacket skins. Once all filled, pop the tray(s) into the freezer to open-freeze the 40 halves for several hours until completely hard, then pack into boxes or freezer bags.

Alternatively, allow the potatoes to cool, then make a cross in the skins and freeze whole, just as they are.

To reheat

When it comes to needing a quick filling meal, microwave 3 potato halves from frozen as follows. Place on a plate, cover with an upturned microwave-proof bowl and cook on High for 3 minutes. Leave in the microwave to rest for 1 minute, then cook for a further 2 minutes. Adjust the microwave times for more or fewer potatoes.

For two whole frozen potatoes, place them on the turntable, cover with an upturned bowl and microwave for 4 minutes. Leave to rest for 1 minute then cook for a further 2 minutes. To check that the potato is piping hot I stick a fork in the middle, take it out, and if the prongs are hot to the touch then it is heated right through. If still cold, microwave an additional minute or two.

BRING ON THE BREAD RECIPES!

My grandmother always made her own bread and I have a fond memory of helping her in the kitchen. She had a huge glazed earthenware proving bowl which she covered simply with a tea towel and left the ball of dough to rise by the fire, turning the bowl from time to time to make sure that the dough didn't get too hot. The soft pillow of dough would then be floured, shaped and popped into the oven to bake. The kitchen would be filled with warmth and gorgeous smells, then my treat was to be given the 'coggy boat' from the end of the loaf, still warm, with butter. Absolutely wonderful.

I decided that if there was only one food left that I could choose to live on forever, mine would be bread. I love making it, eating it fresh and then, because I know how much effort, precious ingredients and expensive energy has gone into producing my loaf, I will not waste a crumb.

Unfortunately, food waste is a big issue, and bread is the single most wasted food – in the UK that's around 20 million slices a day (I read this on Love Food Hate Waste website). Rather than discarding old bread, try to upcycle it and use it to make something delicious. Here are a few ideas, tips and recipes to help you reduce waste and save money.

Small Family or Live Alone?

When you buy your sliced loaf, pop half in the freezer. Once the first half is eaten, the second half can be thawed in less than an hour and will be as fresh as the day it was bought.

For those living alone, freeze the whole sliced loaf and remove one or two slices as required. Frozen slices of bread can easily be separated from the loaf using the blade of a round-ended knife.

If you make your own bread but find it often goes stale before you have had the chance to eat it, cut it in half as soon as it has cooled and freeze half for later.

Stale Bread Breadcrumbs

Processed white sliced bread contains many additives and preservatives and is mostly wrapped in plastic, and for those reasons it often turns mouldy before it feels hard, dry and stale. If you are using factory-made bread and you want to make this or any of the following recipes, keep an eye on it and try to get to it before the mould appears.

Cut into 2.5cm (1in) chunks, then blitz in the bowl of a food processor using the blade attachment. The breadcrumbs in this state will freeze perfectly, so simply place into a bag or box and use from frozen. Home-made bread, on the other hand, tends to go stale (hard) before it goes mouldy and can easily be grated if you don't have a food processor.

Instant Thickener

Adding dry flour or cornflour to a hot casserole or sauce to thicken it will create lumps, so always mix the flour to a paste with a little cold water first before stirring through. Alternatively, use breadcrumbs as a last-minute speedy thickener. Stir in a tablespoon at a time to quickly thicken without fear of lumps.

Instant Crunch

Heat 1–2 tablespoons of oil in a frying pan then sprinkle over a cup of fresh breadcrumbs, a sprinkle of dried garlic and dried herbs and fry until crisp and golden. A tasty instant crunch to top off a shepherd's pie, fish pie, pasta bake, salad or the batch-baked spuds on page 169. Delicious.

Pretend Pizza

Stale bread blitzed to breadcrumbs can be used to knock up what I refer to as my 'pretend pizza', which is actually quite delicious hot or cold. I use up leftover bits from the fridge in the topping and it is a great way to make a budget meal out of ingredients that may otherwise have been thrown away.

You will need

mixing bowl
wooden spoon
23cm (9in) round or 20cm (8in) square, loose-bottomed
    cake tin, flan ring or flan tin lined with reusable baking
    parchment or greaseproof paper
baking sheet

225g (8oz) fresh breadcrumbs
1 egg, beaten
100ml (3½fl oz) water
2–3 tbsp tomato purée
1 tsp dried mixed herbs
130g (4¼oz) grated cheese (any cheese you have)

OPTIONAL TOPPINGS

sliced peppers (fresh or frozen)

1 tbsp olives, pitted and sliced

2 tbsp cooked cubes of ham, cooked bacon or chorizo

Place the breadcrumbs, egg and water into a bowl, stir well, then set aside for 5 minutes to allow the breadcrumbs to soak up the liquid. While this is happening gather together your toppings of choice.

Once the pizza base mix has thickened, take the cake tin, flan tin or ring and spread the breadcrumb mixture into the base, then smooth it with the back of a spoon. Add the tomato purée, leaving just a narrow margin around the edge of the tin, then sprinkle dried mixed herbs over the top. Follow with the grated cheese and any other toppings you may want to add. Chill until ready to bake then preheat the oven to 200°C/180°C fan/400°F/gas 6 with a baking sheet inside. Slide the tin onto the preheated baking sheet and cook in the oven for 20–25 minutes until the cheese is melted, golden and bubbling.

Run a knife around the edges of the tin, then pop the 'pizza' out onto a board, slide the base of the tin away and cut into wedges using a pizza cutter. Serve with salad leaves or on its own.

Shelf Breadcrumbs

Stuck for freezer space? You can dry your breadcrumbs. Spread the fresh breadcrumbs onto a baking tray in a thin layer and place in the oven to dry out. If the oven has been on for something else, pop in the tray of breadcrumbs when you have finished cooking and before the oven cools down. The breadcrumbs, once dried, will feel coarse and will not stick to the hands. For a very fine crumb, blitz again in a blender once dried.

Once cool, dried breadcrumbs can be stored in a jar in a cupboard indefinitely – perfect for coating Scotch eggs, fish cakes, fish fingers, chicken and vegetables.

Canapés

Rather than rush out to buy blinis or unfilled vol-au-vents, use up your bread to make these absolutely delicious canapés. So many times have I made these for parties, pre-dinner nibbles (instead of a starter) and without exception they all get eaten and I am asked for the recipe. Use any medium sliced bread, though I find a seeded or wholemeal bread gives a tastier result.

MAKES 60

You will need

rolling pin
5cm (2in) round metal cutter
24-hole mini muffin tin
small saucepan or microwave-safe bowl
pastry brush
reusable piping bag and star nozzle
food processor

15 slices medium-sliced wholemeal bread
100g (3½oz) butter

3 tsp fennel seeds ground to a powder in a coffee grinder or pestle and mortar, or use 1 tsp garlic powder and 1 tsp paprika, or simply 1 tsp black pepper

Preheat the oven to 200°C/180°C fan/400°F/gas 6. Use the rolling pin to roll the slices of bread flat, then cut four rounds from each slice using the 5cm (2in) cutter. Trimmings left over from the cut-outs can be used to make breadcrumbs.

Melt the butter either in a small saucepan or the microwave, then stir in the flavourings. Fennel works well, as does powdered garlic with paprika or simply black pepper.

Using a pastry brush, coat the insides of each cup of a 24-hole mini muffin tin with the flavoured melted butter. Then line each cup with a bread circle, pressing them down with the end of a mini rolling pin if you have one, or with your hands, then brush them over with the butter. Cook in the oven for 12–15 minutes until the shells are baked, crispy and dark golden brown. Remove to a cooling rack to cool completely.

Once baked the crispy shells (croustades) will keep (unfilled) for up to two weeks in an airtight tin, ready for filling.

Filling ideas

SMOKED MACKEREL
300g (10½oz) smoked mackerel fillets, skin removed
150g (5½oz) soured cream
3 tsp freshly grated horseradish
finely grated zest of 1 lemon
salt and pepper, to taste

finely cut tiny lemon wedge
fresh parsley, dill or chives sprigs
pinch of paprika

To make the filling, simply place all the ingredients in the bowl of a food processor and blitz until you have a smooth paste. Load the mixture into a piping bag fitted with a star nozzle and fill each croustade. Decorate with the tiniest lemon wedge, a sprig of herbs and a pinch of paprika.

SMOKED SALMON
300ml (10fl oz) double cream
100ml (3½fl oz) soured cream
3–4 tbsp creamy horseradish sauce
1 tsp lemon juice
salt and pepper, to taste

TO DECORATE
200g smoked salmon
thinly sliced black olives
fresh parsley or dill sprigs
pomegranate seeds or slices of fresh mild red chilli for
    colour

Whisk the double cream to soft peaks then fold in the soured cream, horseradish sauce, lemon juice and salt and pepper. Load into a piping bag fitted with a star nozzle and fill each croustade. Decorate with a mini roll of smoked salmon, thinly sliced black olive, parsley or dill sprig and a pomegranate seed or chilli slice.

Once filled these canapés will stay fresh and crunchy for 2–3 hours until ready to serve.

Mock Eve's Pudding

Eve's Pudding is a British classic first referenced, I believe, in 1824, and was traditionally made using ground almonds. Ground almonds can nowadays be very expensive. My budget version that omits the nuts still manages to pass the taste test – nobody knew it was topped with old bread when I served it up! The classic version is made with apples, but in the spring I have discovered a fondness for this pudding made with rhubarb, orange and ginger.

SERVES 4

You will need

mixing bowl
hand-held electric whisk
a deep pudding or gratin dish (mine measures 26 x 19 x
    5cm deep/10 x 7.5 x 2in) greased or brushed with lining
    paste (see page 16)
fork or a spoon

125g (4¼oz) soft butter (try home churned – see page 211)
125g (4¼oz) sugar
2 eggs, beaten
125g (4¼oz) fresh breadcrumbs
20g (½oz) self-raising flour (or gluten-free flour)

½ tsp almond extract (or ½ tsp ground ginger for the
  rhubarb version)

FOR AN APPLE PUDDING

450g (1lb) medium dessert or baking apples, peeled and
  thinly sliced (perfect for windfalls!)
2–3 tbsp sugar
2 tbsp flaked almonds (optional)

FOR A RHUBARB, ORANGE AND GINGER PUDDING

500g (1lb 2oz) trimmed rhubarb, cut into 2cm (¾in) pieces
1 orange (the zest and segments)
1 tsp dried ginger (or 1–2 tbsp grated frozen ginger, see
  page 155)

This pudding will wait in the fridge until you are ready to put
the oven on for something else. The oven temperature needs
to be 160–170°C/140–150°C fan/320–340°F/gas 3 and it will
bake perfectly alongside a casserole or whatever else you're
planning for tea that evening.

Start by mixing the batter. Place all the ingredients into a
large mixing bowl then mix together with an electric hand
whisk until well combined and thick.

For the apple pudding, place the sliced apples in the prepared
pudding tin, or if making the rhubarb version, add all the
ingredients to the tin and mix to distribute the flavours. For
the apple version, sprinkle over the sugar immediately (before
the apples start to go brown), then spoon the batter over the
top. Spread over the fruit base using a fork or the back of a
spoon, then sprinkle over the flaked almonds, if using.

Serve with the Egg-free Custard on page 194.

TIP: If your pudding starts to over-brown before the end of the cooking time, turn the oven from fan to conventional cooking. Turning off the fan will ensure that the sheet of foil you are about to lay over will not blow off the pudding. Then place a piece of foil with a hole in the centre (the hole about the size of a cup) over the pudding. This will allow the centre to continue to brown but will protect the edges.

BREAD BOOSTERS

Nothing beats the taste, smell and texture of freshly baked bread, though I know not everyone has the time to set aside for bread baking. However, I have included the following low- or no-cost 'boosters', which will enhance the flavour, texture and proving of your home-baked loaf.

Create Your Own (Minimal Energy) Proving Oven

Bread needs a warm, humid environment to prove to its very best, and some modern ovens have a setting that will do that for you. I have a 'dough proving' setting with my oven which I am not too enamoured with, as the air circulation while the oven is on creates a dry crust to the dough. In addition, the dough needs to be removed prior to switching on the oven for baking. If you want to prove your dough with no inter-ruption, use less energy, or if you have no proving oven and a cold kitchen like mine, resulting in your bread proving being a bit hit and miss, then try this little tip. It will prove your bread in the best environment using minimal energy – though you do need a microwave.

Pop half a cup of water into the microwave and run on High for 1–2 minutes until you see the water in the cup start to bubble and boil. Turn off the microwave. Place your tin of shaped bread into the microwave alongside the cup of steaming water, close the door immediately to keep the steam in, and leave to prove, uncovered. The warm, steam-filled, sealed, micro-wave oven box will provide the perfect conditions for your rising dough and reduce the proving time considerably. I leave mine for 30 minutes to prove before baking.

An alternative would be to place a cup of boiling water in an oven with only the light on, which gives off very minimal heat, though of course you will need to take the dough and water out of the oven before pre-heating for the bake.

Don't salt your spuds!

If you are boiling potatoes and are considering making any bread, don't salt your spuds. Boil your potatoes as normal but without salt, adding it afterwards. Strain off the water into a jug, leave to cool, then use this in place of the water needed in your bread recipe. The potato 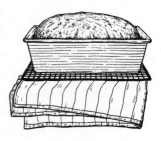 starch will give the yeast a huge boost – they are great pals – and see your bread rise. If not used within about 24 hours the potato water discolours, so I tend not to keep it for long.

MY PERFECT PASTRY TOP TIPS TO ENSURE TOP-END TARTS

I have included my two favourite (budget) tart recipes here that don't cost the earth but certainly have the 'wow' factor and look as though they do! Both recipes require that the pastry be blind baked (pre-baked), and to achieve a professional tidy 'top-end' looking tart the secret to success is having my two blind baking tips up your sleeve. Pastry is patient and will sit happily in the fridge for a day until the oven goes on for something else, and of course it loves the freezer!

Pastry is easy and cheap to make, yet so many people are frightened of it and decide instead to buy a block of ready-made processed dough. Take a minute to read the number of ingredients in that plastic-packed, perfectly formed block – I think there were eleven when I last looked, compared to just four or five for home-made. When it comes to taste, nothing beats home-made.

It is no mistake that I have used imperial measurements (lbs and ozs) for my pastry dough recipe. Working this way I can accurately calculate the amounts I need. I use half fat to flour and to then calculate the amount of liquid to be used for my dough, I know that for every ounce of fat used I need 1 tablespoon of liquid. For example, in this recipe you will see I have used 8oz flour and half fat is 4oz butter. For the liquid, I therefore need 4 tablespoons, which in this recipe consists of one egg yolk (being my first tablespoon) and the other three are water.

It is simple and it works. For those new to pastry making,

coming across a recipe that suggests simply adding sufficient water to form a dough – how on earth can you begin to know? The correct amount of liquid is the secret to success when it comes to pastry.

||||||||||||||||||||||||||||||||||||||||||||||||||||||||||||||||||||||||||||||||||||||||||||||||||||||||||||||||||||||||||||||||

TIP: Save cereal-packet liners and upcycle to use as freezer bags, sandwich bags, wrappers for food in the fridge or to store pastry trimmings, to be then opened out and used to help roll out pastry dough, which with the following blind baking tips will turn your leftover pastry waste into top-end tarts!

||||||||||||||||||||||||||||||||||||||||||||||||||||||||||||||||||||||||||||||||||||||||||||||||||||||||||||||||||||||||||||||||

MAKES 400G BLOCK OF PASTRY DOUGH. THIS IS A STANDARD BATCH – 250G OF THIS WILL MAKE 12 TARTS, THEN YOU CAN FREEZE THE REST.

You will need

food processor with blade attachment
large roomy mixing bowl if mixing by hand
round-bladed knife (for hand mixing)
reused cereal packet liner, beeswax wrap or greaseproof
    paper

FOR THE DOUGH
8oz plain flour, plus extra for dusting
4oz chilled butter cut into cubes (for machine) or room-
    temperature butter if mixing by hand

pinch of salt

1 egg yolk mixed with 3 tbsp cold water

By machine

Add the flour, cubed butter and salt to the bowl of the food processor with the blade attachment. Blitz for about 10 seconds until the mixture in the bowl resembles breadcrumbs.

With the motor running, pour the egg and water mixture down the feeder tube in a thin, steady stream and leave the machine to do the rest. In around 30 seconds the dough will form itself into a ball. Turn off the machine, turn out the ball of dough onto the worktop, shape lightly and wrap in one of the pieces of cereal-packet liner (or use cloth, beeswax wrap or greaseproof paper). Pop into the fridge to rest and firm up for 30 minutes.

By hand

Place the flour, room-temperature butter and salt into the large mixing bowl. After washing my hands I then rinse mine in cold water – pastry dough hates the heat. Using your fingertips, rub the fat into the flour until it forms rough breadcrumbs. My grandmother's words constantly ring in my ears: 'light hand for pastry and heavy hand for bread.' Lightly does it – gently rub that fat into the flour, don't bang and knead it as you would do with bread dough.

When the mix resembles breadcrumbs, pour over the egg and water mix and use the round-bladed knife to help clump the dough together before finally taking a hand to it and working it until it forms a ball. Knead lightly on a lightly floured work surface, and because the liquid has been calculated accurately it should be neither too sticky nor too dry – just right.

Transfer to a sheet of plastic liner (or use cloth, beeswax wrap or greaseproof paper) and pop it into the fridge to rest and firm up for 30 minutes, or freeze as it is for later use. Uncooked pastry dough can be refrozen, by the way; if I have taken a ball of dough from the freezer and used it for a tart, I save the trimmings in a bag and refreeze them until I have sufficient pastry to make something else.

Jam and Lemon Curd Tarts

I love a jam or lemon curd tart, but until I came up with this tip I could never get them to look appealing. The tarts would bubble up in the oven, spill over the edge of the pastry and then glue the pastry shell to the tin – a complete mess. I remember this idea once coming to me in the middle of the night, and I was up the next day at a ridiculously early hour to give it a try.

This method will ensure you have the perfect jam or lemon curd tarts.

MAKES 12 TARTS

You will need

2 sheets food-grade plastic (I reuse cereal packet liners) or
    use greaseproof paper
rolling pin
8cm (3in) fluted cutter
2 identical 12-hole tart tins, one brushed with lining paste
    (see page 16) in the holes as normal and the other
    brushed ever so lightly on the underside of the cups
microwave-safe jug
spoon

250g (9oz) shortcrust pastry
350g (12oz) your favourite jam or
    bought lemon curd
    or Minute Lemon Curd (see
    page 221), plus 3–4 tbsp
    water

Lay out a sheet of greaseproof paper or a cereal packet liner that has been opened out to make one large sheet. Place the ball of pastry dough on top, flatten it with the heel of your hand, then cover with the second sheet.

Take the rolling pin and begin to roll the dough – starting from the middle and working outwards. The advantage of having the dough within the two sheets is that it can be lifted, moved, twisted and messed around with without the need for extra flour (which will toughen the finished crust) – and no sticking, no fingers poking through and no overheating. If at any time you need to pause to do something else, or you feel the dough is becoming too warm, just slide the covered dough onto a baking sheet and pop into the fridge for 10 minutes.

Continue to roll out the dough until you achieve a circle around 30cm (12in) in diameter at a thickness of about a £1 coin. At this stage, pop it into the fridge for 10 minutes to firm up.

In the meantime, preheat the oven to 200°C/180°C fan/400°F/gas 6.

Take the chilled rolled-out dough from the fridge, and once on the work surface peel off the top sheet. Use the cutter to cut out 12 rounds, re-rolling the dough if necessary. Peel the rounds from the bottom sheet. If they stick at all, pop them back into the fridge on the sheet for 5 minutes – they should then peel away cleanly. Gently mould the dough shells into the greased holes of the tart tin. I use the end of the rolling pin rather than my fingers to ease them into the base, then there is no fear of the dough cracking. If the oven is not yet to temperature, pop the tray into the fridge while you wait. The fridge is your friend when it comes to pastry making.

When ready to bake, take the second identical tart tin – the bottom of the cups have been slightly greased to prevent them sticking to the shells. Lay the second tray over the chilled shells very gently and without pushing it down. Slide into the preheated oven and bake for 12 minutes – I am erring on the side of caution here because all ovens vary and it is not possible to see what is going on.

When the baking time is up, remove the two trays to a heatproof surface and carefully lift off the top tray. The pastry shells need to be golden brown and baked through. If the shells need a little more colour, look grey and waxy at the base, pop them back into the oven as they are (don't cover again) for 3–4 minutes. You could even turn the oven off and use the residual heat for free. Leave the cooked pastry shells in the tin to cool while you prepare the filling.

Transfer the jam to a microwave-safe jug and add the water (for a flavour boost, try adding 1–2 tablespoons of elderflower cordial, too, if you have it), stir, then microwave in 30-second bursts, stirring between each session until the jam becomes hot and can be poured. Carefully fill each warm pastry shell to the brim with the runny jam, then leave to cool – it will re-set completely, and then the tarts can be removed from the tins.

For lemon curd tarts, heat the bought lemon curd in a pan with water or use the microwave as for jam. Or you can make your own lemon curd 'in a minute' – see Minute Lemon Curd on page 221. Pour into the tarts while still runny and hot. The lemon curd will set in the pastry shells once cold.

There you have it – top-end (yet budget) tarts! These tarts will be devoured instantly, I promise, but if not they will keep in an airtight tin for at least a week.

Strawberry Cups

Serve up these jaw-dropping beauties, fit to be displayed in the window of any French patisserie, in the knowledge that they have cost very little to make, especially if you use leftover egg yolks as well as leftover pastry.

Unlike the traditional jam tarts described above, these deep-filled cups are blind baked in a muffin tin. If you have ever struggled to blind bake a deep, small cup such as this – and the job of then removing them from the tin is even more difficult – try this easy method. You need to buy ridged paper fairy cake cases (smaller than muffin cases) and you will find that they work magic on your pastry if you follow these simple instructions.

MAKES 12

You will need

pastry brush
rolling pin
9cm (4in) fluted pastry cutter
12-hole deep muffin tin
12 paper fairy cake cases (from the shop, smaller than
    muffin cases)

lentils
baking sheet
medium mixing bowl
hand-held electric whisk
piping bag and large star nozzle

lining paste (see page 16)
250g (9oz) shortcrust pastry
400g (14oz) No-faff Crème Pâtissière (see page 224)
300ml (10fl oz) double or whipping cream
2 tbsp icing sugar
12 strawberries

Brush the deep cups of the tin with lining paste. Roll out the pastry as for the jam tarts (see page 188), then cut out 12 circles using the 9cm (4in) fluted pastry cutter. Using the end of the rolling pin as an aid, line each hole with the pastry cut-out. There's no need to flour the end of the pin; take the cut-out shell, gently mould around the end of the wooden pin using the palm of your hand, then ease it into the base of the tin. A gentle twist and the pin will leave the dough.

Once each cup is lined, pop the tray into the fridge to firm up for 10–15 minutes. When working with pastry, the fridge is your friend. Pastry dough hates feeling hot, so at any opportunity, pop it into the fridge rather than leaving it out on a work surface.

For blind baking, the oven needs to be at a temperature of 200°C/180°C fan/400°F/gas 6. So often a recipe calls for the oven to be preheated before starting, but I think that can lead to an unnecessary waste of valuable energy, especially if the oven is ready before you are. I would much prefer to finish my baking prep and then chill my pastry, scones or biscuits, then switch on the oven, so while it comes to temperature my pastry is given a further opportunity to firm up – much better for pastry baking.

In addition, there is not the added stress of having to work quickly if the oven is ready before you are, and you feel yourself getting hot and bothered – the oven is spending your money running on empty, and then the phone rings or someone comes to the door, which makes things even worse. I turn the oven on when I'm ready – the pastry is chilled, and so am I.

Take the chilled pastry from the fridge, then line each cup with a paper fairy cake case so it fits perfectly, gently pushing the ridges of the case into the sides of the dough. Fill each case right to the top with lentils (which can be kept in a box along with the paper cases and used over and over again). The lentils will keep the pastry shell in place while it is baking.

Pop the whole lot into the oven and bake for 12–15 minutes, until the top edge of the visible pastry has baked to a golden brown colour.

Remove from the oven, use your hands to gently pull on the edges of the paper case, and (this is the miraculous part) the paper and the pastry shell will release together from the hot tin. The baked pastry shell, paper case and lentils are all in one piece and at this point they should be transferred to the cold baking sheet. This can only be done while the pastry is hot; if left to cool in the tin the paper will leave the pastry shell.

Once out of the tin and onto the baking sheet, leave to cool slightly then use the paper again as an aid – carefully peel one edge of the paper from the pastry and you will see how easy it now is to lift the lentil-filled cases away from the cooked shell. The baked pastry shells need to look completely baked, pale golden in colour and dry to the touch. If the pastry looks grey and waxy at the base, pop it back into the oven for a further 5 minutes, still on the baking sheet, to complete the bake.

Make the two-minute No-faff Crème Pâtissière (page 224). When the crème pâtissière is freshly made and hot it can be poured into the cooling pastry shells. If it is cold because it was made in advance, it is easier to spoon in and smooth over with the back of a teaspoon.

Whisk the cream to soft peaks or to a consistency that just drops off the whisk when lifted up. Adding in the icing sugar will help to prevent over-whipping. Transfer the cream to a piping bag fitted with a large star nozzle and pipe a swirl over each tart, covering over the layer of crème pâtissière, then top off each with a fresh strawberry.

EGG-FREE CUSTARD

My go-to for a quick microwave custard is Bird's custard powder (it's been around for two hundred years, I think, and was originally developed by Alfred Bird because his wife was allergic to eggs). However, I know it is not readily available to all. If you can't get it, have run out, want to save money and make it for less, or vary the flavour and colour, then we can make our own. Kids love colourful custard.

Remember chocolate pudding with pink custard at school? Making this simple pouring custard works out cheaper than buying custard powders or sachets and is a great option for the gluten-free and vegans around the table.

You will need

1 litre (34fl oz) microwave-safe jug or small saucepan

2 tbsp cornflour
2–3 tsp sugar
1 tsp vanilla extract
2–3 drops of food colour of choice (yellow for a traditional pouring custard)
400ml (14fl oz) whole milk (works perfectly with oat, soya and almond milks)

TIP: For a chocolate custard, add 1 tbsp cocoa powder to the cornflour, leaving out any colouring, and for a brandy or rum sauce at Christmas time add 1 tbsp rum or brandy (or to taste!), omitting any colouring.

Measure the cornflour, sugar, vanilla and food colour into a microwave-safe jug (I use a Pyrex one then I can see what is going on). For a smooth, lump-free custard, stir 4 tablespoons of the milk into the cornflour mix in order to make a smooth but thick paste, then add the rest of the milk and stir to combine.

Pop into the microwave on full power for 2 minutes, stirring halfway through. It may need a few seconds more, but once you see the custard start to rise up the sides of the jug it will be thickened and ready to serve.

If you don't have a microwave, simply mix everything together, then heat the ingredients in a small saucepan on the stove top or hob.

GOLDEN SYRUP

Delicious golden syrup has been around as long as I can remember and is used in many British baking recipes. Not to be confused with corn syrup or honey, as the flavour is quite unique. It is simply a sugar syrup cooked for the right length of time to give it just the right colour along with that distinctive slight caramel flavour, yet it remains thick and able to be spooned. If it's not cooked for long enough it will not have that golden hue and will be too thin and runny once cooled; yet cooked for too long it will be nearly brown in colour, and will set hard and taste bitter.

When I discovered that golden syrup can be made at home using just three ingredients and, more importantly, for a quarter of the price of popular brands, and tastes the same and keeps indefinitely – what's not to like? Also, stored in a glass jar you will not be left with the tell-tale rust rings on the pantry shelf, which always seems to happen. The tins are attractive and nostalgic, though, so if you prefer to treasure your tin, pop your home-made golden syrup in there. No one will ever know.

There is the energy cost to consider, but even after factoring in about an hour on the lowest setting on the hob or stove top, even my maths tells me that the price of your jar of golden syrup is still significantly reduced.

In addition, I know many non-UK readers find it difficult to access golden syrup and have to either pay exorbitant prices or do without.

You will need

small or medium stainless-steel saucepan
small spatula
jam funnel (optional)
2 x 450g (1lb) clean jars with lids

400g (14oz) granulated sugar
150ml (5fl oz) water
1 tbsp lemon juice

Place the sugar and water in the saucepan. It's best to use a stainless-steel type saucepan, i.e. without a black non-stick coating, as it is essential that you can see the colour of the syrup. Place over a medium heat and stir once or twice until the sugar dissolves and the syrup is clear.

Bring to the boil then turn the heat down to its lowest setting and simmer for 50 minutes to 1 hour. The syrup needs to just bubble very slowly, with a very steady stream of bubbles rising from the base to the surface, at a very slow simmer, no rising up the sides of the pan – just a gentle ticking over. After 30 minutes the syrup will begin to change colour from clear to a pale straw colour. Do not stir, just keep an eager eye on it. Heat the jars in the oven or the microwave to sterilize them (see page 223).

If in any doubt at any time about the colour, turn off the heat, allow the syrup to calm down, then examine it. A rich golden colour is what you are aiming for and if you know golden syrup you recognize the colour. If it is still a bit pale, on with the heat again for a further 5 minutes.

When happy with the finished hue – a rich mid-golden/orange colour – pour it into the two warm glass jars and seal. Even though the syrup may seem very runny it will thicken and firm up once cold.

It can be used in many budget baking recipes. Children (and adults) like a drizzle on porridge and rice pudding and you can use it to make flapjack or try my low-energy/high-energy 'no-bake' bars (see page 201).

CHERRY AND COCONUT FLAPJACK

The cost of baking this nostalgic treat is much reduced if using home-made golden syrup. I am a fan of flapjack because it is easy, everything is mixed in the saucepan, the unbaked flapjack will sit in the fridge for a day or two until the oven goes on and, once baked, cooled and cut into slices, it will keep in a tin for at least two weeks.

Flapjack is one of those nostalgic bakes that many people adore, but when I see the high price that is charged for a single serving of the factory produced, plastic-wrapped (excessively sweet) version in many supermarkets, motorway services and cafes, this seemed a perfect fit for this book.

Just as an aside, though I consider a home-made flapjack and cereal bar to enjoy a long shelf life, I urge you to examine the best-before date on the factory produced versions. The one I bought had a date two months hence – I wonder what chemicals, additives and preservatives have gone into those?

MAKES 16 PIECES

You will need

> medium saucepan or use a microwave-safe bowl
> wooden spoon, angled palette knife or spatula
> oblong tin about 4cm (1½in) deep – mine measures 26cm x 18cm (10 x 7in)
> a piece of reusable baking parchment or greaseproof paper to line the tin
> sharp knife

100g (3½oz) margarine or butter

3 tbsp golden syrup (bought or home-made, see page 196)

100g (3½oz) demerara sugar

40g (1½oz) desiccated coconut

160g (5½oz) porridge oats

1 tsp almond extract (brings out the cherry flavour)

80g (3oz) glacé cherries, chopped – about 12 (I use morello glacé, cherries which are darker and packed with flavour)

|||||||||||||||||||||||||||||||||||||||||||||||||||||||||||||||||||||||||||||||||||||||||||||||||||||||||||||||||||||||||

TIP: Make a plain flapjack costing even less by omitting the cherries, almond extract and coconut and increasing the porridge oats to 280g (10oz).

|||||||||||||||||||||||||||||||||||||||||||||||||||||||||||||||||||||||||||||||||||||||||||||||||||||||||||||||||||||||||

Flapjack is not fussy at all. It will sit in the fridge until the oven goes on and will happily bake alongside your dinner – slide it into a space on any shelf. The temperature needs to be between 180°C/160°C fan/350°F/gas 4 and 200°C/180°C fan/400°F/gas 6.

In a medium saucepan melt the margarine or butter and golden syrup – don't allow the mixture to boil. Alternatively, heat them in a bowl in the microwave for around 30 seconds or until the butter melts. Remove from the heat, then stir in the sugar, then the coconut and finally the oats, almond extract and cherries. Mix well so that all the dry ingredients have absorbed the moisture.

Transfer to the prepared tin and smooth with the back of a spoon or an angled palette knife.

Bake in the oven for 20–25 minutes until golden brown.

Leave for 5 minutes, then with a sharp knife or pizza cutter mark out 16 pieces.

Leave to cool completely then remove from the tin, peel off the parchment and the flapjack can be cut or broken along the score lines.

Will keep in an airtight tin for up to two weeks.

High-energy/Low-energy 'No-Bake' Bars

For the same reasons I have included the flapjack recipe above, using the budget golden syrup, I couldn't help thinking home-made cereal bars are great for those 'on the go' – for a packed lunch or quick snack – and these tasty bites always go down a treat.

When I think about the number of times I have grabbed a mass-produced bar from a kiosk at the railway station just to keep me going until I got home. A home-made version is so much better on many fronts – cost, nutrition, no plastic packaging (wrap a home-made one in a beeswax wrap or greaseproof paper) and is much more tasty! You also know exactly what has gone into them and, the best bit, there's no need for the oven or the hob as there's no baking involved!

MAKES 16

You will need

food processor with blade attachment
large microwave-safe mixing bowl
oblong tin about 4cm (1½in) deep – mine measures 26cm x
   18cm (10 x7in) – or 23cm (9in) square tin
reusable baking parchment

wooden spoon, angled palette knife or spatula
large knife
chopping board

260g (9oz) porridge oats
30g (1oz) cocoa powder
180g (6oz) butter or coconut oil (or a combination of both)
160g (5½oz) golden syrup
1–2 tsp ground cinnamon
½ tsp salt
150g (5½oz) mix of chopped nuts and seeds
150g (5½oz) mix of dried fruits or desiccated coconut

So that the finished bars can be cut into neat pieces, I prefer to avoid any huge lumps in the mixture. I firstly blitz the porridge oats and cocoa together to a fairly fine crumb, then roughly chop any large nuts and fruits. All of this can be done in the food processor with the blade attached.

In the large mixing bowl, microwave together the butter or oil and golden syrup until liquid, about 30 seconds. Add the blitzed oats and cocoa and stir well, then once you've used the processor to blitz the fruit and nuts, add those in too along with the cinnamon, salt, nuts and seeds and dried fruits or coconut.

Mix very thoroughly, then spread into an even layer in the tin, pressing down firmly and smoothing out with the back of a spoon or angled palette knife. Pop into the fridge and leave overnight to firm up completely.

Next day, take the tin from the fridge, lift the solid bar from the tin using the paper or parchment as an aid. Peel off the parchment, transfer to a wooden board and cut into 16 even-sized bars.

Will keep in an airtight tin for up to 2 weeks, and in warm weather I store these bars in the fridge to keep them hard.

CARROTS

Carrots are available all the year round in the shops and supermarkets and are easy to grow, too. They are one of my favourite colourful veggies and as they are filled with beta carotene and lots of vitamins they are one of the healthiest additions to our winter diet. They are not expensive and can be used in so many everyday recipes, as well as being delicious raw in salads and a colourful addition to dips. Whether it's stews, casseroles, soups, stocks, jam or cake – don't forget the carrots.

||||||||||||||||||||||||||||||||||||||||||||||||||||||||||||||||||||||||||||||||||||||||||||||||||||||||||||

TIPS: Slice thinly, drizzle with oil and air-fry,
microwave or oven bake into crisps (see page 238).
Or carrot peelings are perfect for a quick stock
(see page 240).

||||||||||||||||||||||||||||||||||||||||||||||||||||||||||||||||||||||||||||||||||||||||||||||||||||||||||||

Carrot Soup

Carrot soup is such a thrifty meal and I often smile to myself when I see it on the list of starters in restaurants. Rarely referred to as simply 'carrot soup' – it'll be made to sound much more appealing with the addition of ginger, coriander or orange – but the real hero is the carrot. Carrots are tasty and once cooked will blitz to a smooth soup with no extra thickening required. A fantastic vegan, vegetarian, gluten-free and low-fat food. If I see a bargain bag of carrots, I will make a batch as it freezes really well.

Carrots produce a delicious creamy soup with a hearty flavour. Make on the hob, in a slow cooker or quickly in a pressure cooker. Low-calorie, low-fat and yummy. You can also add a touch of zing as mentioned by simply adding a few optional extras as follows.

SERVES 6

You will need

vegetable knife
chopping board
large microwave-safe bowl if making the quick stock, with a
    lid or plate to cover
large saucepan, pressure cooker or slow cooker
wooden spoon or spatula
hand blender or liquidizer

1 large onion
1kg (2lb 4oz) carrots
1 celery stick (if you don't have celery use 2 tsp celery salt –
    a handy dried jar to have on the shelf)
2 cloves of garlic, sliced, or use ½ tsp garlic granules
2 tbsp dried mixed herbs
25g (1oz) butter or oil
1 litre (34fl oz) stock (use chicken stock, dissolve a stock
    cube in a litre of boiling water, or make a quick stock
    from peelings, see page 240)
salt and pepper, to taste

OPTIONAL ADDITIONS:

Carrot and Ginger: 2 tbsp finely grated fresh ginger
    (see freezer ginger on page 155) or 1 tbsp ground
    ginger
Carrot and Coriander: 1 tsp ground coriander – if you
    have fresh I use the stalks in the stock for the soup
    and a few leaves to garnish
Carrot and Orange: Finely grated zest and juice of
    1 medium orange

Finely chop the peeled onions (see notes on page 158), thinly slice the celery, garlic and carrots – smaller pieces take less energy and time to cook.

In the large saucepan, melt and heat the butter or oil, then add the onion and fry until softened (about 5 minutes). Add the chopped celery, carrots and garlic, salt and pepper and one of the flavour pairings mentioned above, if using. Stir thoroughly, then add the hot stock – if you have made the quick stock, simply pour it from the bowl into the pan, straining it through a colander set over the pan.

Bring to the boil on the hob, turn down the heat and simmer gently, covered, for 20–25 minutes until the carrots are tender. If you are cooking in a slow cooker, cook for about 2 hours until the carrots are tender, and in a pressure cooker, for 10 minutes on High pressure.

Leave to cool slightly then blend thoroughly with a stick blender or liquidizer until the soup is thick, smooth and hearty. Taste and adjust the salt and pepper if needed.

Keeps in the fridge in an airtight container for 5 days, or freeze for up to 6 months.

Carrot Jam

Carrot jam is not new, in fact I developed this recipe from one printed by Mrs Beeton back in 1859 or thereabouts. She was an English journalist, editor and writer and is particularly associated with her bumper book *Mrs Beeton's Book of Household Management*.

When I read in there that carrot jam could easily be mistaken for apricot jam (which is very expensive to buy), I just had to give it a go. Mrs Beeton added brandy to her carrot jam to extend the shelf life, back in the day before fridges. I have to say I didn't like the aftertaste the alcohol gave. I prefer instead to keep it in the fridge after making. Mine sat happily in the fridge for 3 weeks, after which time it had all been eaten. I ate it on toast, added a spoonful or two to my uncooked carrots before oven cooking – unbelievably tasty – and served it up in place of apricot jam in an almond tart, nobody knew!

MAKES 2 JARS

You will need

potato peeler
knife
chopping board
medium saucepan
colander
hand blender or food processor
bowl
digital weighing scales

lemon zester

2 clean sterilized 1lb (500g) jars with lids

500g (1lb 2oz) carrots (small ones if you can, without a
   core)
sugar (see note below)
finely grated zest of 1 lemon
1 tsp almond extract

If the carrots are young and without blemish, simply wash the
skins then chop into small round pieces. If the carrots are old,
scrub the skins and remove any blemishes, or peel using the
potato peeler. Cut into small slices. Pop them into the pan
then add sufficient water just to cover. Bring to the boil and
simmer, partially covered, until the carrots are very tender.
Drain, then blitz to a very smooth, thick purée using the hand
blender or food processor.

Place the bowl onto the digital scales, set it to zero then
transfer the carrot pulp into the bowl to weigh it. Whatever
the weight – around 500g (1lb 2oz) – you need the same
amount of sugar (pretty standard for all jams). Transfer the
pulp back into the pan and add the weight of sugar needed.
Over a low heat, stir the two together until the sugar dissolves
and the jam begins to bubble. Keep stirring for 5 minutes,
then take off the heat and leave to cool slightly before adding
the lemon zest and almond extract. Stir well, then transfer into
clean sterilized jars (see page 223 for quick microwave sterilizing) and cover with a lid.

Once completely cold, have a taste! Apricot or carrot?

GETTING AHEAD: NO TIME TODAY!

I have found myself in this situation so many times, particularly when I have leftovers that need using up that I want to pile into a pie, or maybe slices of apple, a picking of soft berries or fruits. The pie fillings need to be in a pie but I don't have the time (or the inclination) to set to and make pastry today! This handy tip has the pie filling done and ready to be finished, with the pastry constructed speedily later on another day.

Gather together your pie filling ingredients; sweeten fruits or peel, slice and dust apples in sugar, or maybe cook and cool any other leftovers you had destined for a pie later. I use a good old cereal packet liner or freezer bag (cut down one side and across the bottom to give a single layer of food-grade plastic) to then lay over my favourite pie dish, tin or plate. Spoon over the cold pie filling of choice or cold cooked or uncooked fruits, smooth over, then pop into the freezer.

Once frozen, fold the excess cereal packet liner or plastic sheet over the frozen filling, remove the pie dish, pop the filling into a freezer bag or box, label and put back into the freezer until you are ready to make pastry.

The day you decide to make your pie, roll out the pastry, line the tin, then retrieve the frozen filling and unwrap. The frozen block is moulded to the shape of the tin so it will fit perfectly. Cover with a pastry lid, then you can bake from frozen or assemble in advance and leave in the fridge to thaw slowly so it's ready to bake later on.

To avoid a soggy bottom to any pie, sprinkle 1–2 tablespoons of ground rice or semolina over the pastry base before adding the filling and top crust. Always chill a pie before baking and as the oven preheats, and heat the baking sheet too, then you can pop the chilled pie straight onto the hot baking sheet, so the pastry base will cook and bake quickly.

THE DOUBLE CREAM PANIC BUY – MAKE YOUR OWN BUTTER

I am as guilty as the next person when it comes to double cream. Whether it be Christmas, Easter or a family gathering, it always seems that I buy too much double cream. As I am then so often left with a surplus and I have a carton or two fast approaching its use-by date, what is to be done?

Double cream can be whipped up, piped into rosettes on greaseproof paper, frozen and then packed into boxes to be popped onto a dessert or cake later, but my go-to for leftover cream is both budget-friendly and guaranteed to be used – butter!

This tip derives from a school lesson around sixty years ago. Back in the day, each primary school child was given a bottle of 'school milk' – full cream in a small 200ml (7fl oz) glass bottle – at playtime every day. This particular day Mr Lucas invited us back into the classroom after collecting our bottle of milk, before we all charged outside to play. Each pupil was told to pour just the cream from the top of their milk into a large glass jar. We then ran outside to play and enjoy our milk before the bell rang for us to come back into class.

The jar of 'top of milk' cream was then sealed with a screw top and passed around for everyone to give it a jolly good shake. By the time it got to me there were yellow blobs beginning to show in the liquid. We each had to explain what we could see, and by the time it got to the last pupil a large piece of butter had formed, which was floating in a pool of residual liquid – buttermilk.

This was such an exciting lesson, and one that has remained with me for all these years. The butter was taken from the jar, popped into a dish and we each spread a Ritz cracker with our own free butter. It was amazing.

Fast-forward to our leftover double cream – let's make butter.

A 300ml (10fl oz) carton of double cream will yield around 200g (7oz) unsalted butter – and by the way, a 300ml (10fl oz) carton of double cream is cheaper than 200g (7oz) salted butter, so if you have the time and the inclination and want something to do for free in front of the TV, become a butter churner. For every 300ml (10fl oz) double cream there will also be a 100ml (3½fl oz) yield of buttermilk, which is great as a substitute for water for bread making and also the perfect ingredient for simple scones. No energy required here – just your own.

You will need

500ml (17fl oz) glass jar with well-fitting screw top
kitchen paper
butter dish or greaseproof paper

300ml (10fl oz) double cream
pinch of salt

OPTIONAL FLAVOUR ADDITIONS
2 cloves of garlic, crushed, or ½ tsp dried garlic, 1–2 tsp
    finely chopped fresh herbs or 1 tsp dried mixed herbs

Pour the cream into the jar, screw on the lid and shake. The cream will thicken at first as it does when whipping, but it will then begin to look curdled before separating out completely to a ball of gorgeous butter floating in a pool of buttermilk. The process takes about 10 minutes.

The butter is soft after 'home churning', so I find it better to put the whole sealed jar into the fridge for fifteen minutes so that the butter firms up. Once lightly chilled, it can easily be taken from the jar using a spoon and dried off on kitchen paper, then you can add salt and/or flavourings if required or leave as unsalted.

Wooden butter shapers are available, but I don't have these, and instead wrap my slab of butter in greaseproof paper then use a small rolling pin to pat it into shape. Once you have a block-shaped piece of butter, pop the parcel into the fridge to firm up completely, then it is ready to enjoy.

It is recommended that home churned butter be rinsed in iced water to remove any residual buttermilk before then drying on kitchen paper. This helps the keeping qualities of the butter and prevents it going rancid. If I am simply home churning a small amount of cream I skip this step, ensuring I pat my butter dry before wrapping, and it keeps in the fridge for 2–3 weeks.

This is such a great use for excess cream, and if I see double cream on the reduced shelf in the supermarket, I grab it.

SCONES

I love this little bake, and like any scone, they can be made in a jiffy. They can be made and topped with home-churned butter followed by jam, of course, but I also enjoy them with a slice of cheese. I always make scones by hand – over-working by machine can result in a poor rise and tough crumb.

MAKES 6

You will need

sieve
mixing bowl
round-bladed knife
rolling pin
5cm (2in) cutter
baking sheet lightly greased with butter, lining paste (see
    page 16) or lined with reusable baking parchment

225g (8oz) self-raising flour, plus extra for dusting
½ tsp baking powder
50g (1¾oz) (home-churned) butter at room temperature,
    cut into dice
35g (1oz) caster or granulated sugar
1 tsp vanilla extract
100ml (3½fl oz) (home-produced) buttermilk

Preheat the oven to 220°C/200°C fan/425°F/gas 7 if you are cooking straight after making the dough.

Sift the flour into a bowl with the baking powder. Rub in the butter using your fingertips until the mixture resembles breadcrumbs, then stir in the sugar using the round-bladed knife. Use the knife to make a well in the centre, then add the vanilla followed by half of the buttermilk. I use the knife to stir the mix until it begins to clump into large pieces. Add more buttermilk until the dough begins to stick together. The dough needs to be stickier than pastry but not so sticky that you need lots of flour in order to be able to work with it.

Use your hands to bring the dough together into a large ball, then transfer to a lightly floured surface. Handle this dough as little as possible – roll it out to about 1.5cm (½in) thick then cut out 6 scones using the 5cm (2in) cutter and transfer them to the baking sheet, reshaping the trimmings as necessary.

TIP: Flour the cutter between each scone,
then they will release easily.

Brush the tops of the scones with a little leftover buttermilk. Bake for 12–15 minutes until well risen and golden, or pop the unbaked scones in the fridge until the oven goes on for something else. Best eaten the same day as baking.

THE MICROWAVE –
GETTING THERE
QUICKER AND
CHEAPER

can remember the time, for me back in the 1980s, when the word microwave was on everyone's lips. This new piece of kit had the ability to drastically change our kitchen life. In the beginning, these very mysterious boxes were so expensive. I bought a basic model from the low end of the market. No adjustments could be made, no controls to speak of, only a timer and an on/off switch. My friend, on the other hand, bought the 'best' one on the market, with lots of adjustments, a handy cooking calculator, it weighed the food going in and could defrost too – but it was also five times the price of mine.

I remember our excitement; we joined a microwave cooking class and every week the food prepared and demonstrated would then be raffled off. I won the microwaved Black Forest Gateau one week – there's a 1980s favourite for you!

The microwave, over the decades, has been used less and less, because there are no doubt certain foods that do not cook as well and, as we all know, a minute or two too long and the food can be ruined. In addition, unlike conventional cooking, no attractive caramelizing or browning takes place. However, the microwave continues to be the cheapest cooking appliance and there are a number of kitchen tasks where the microwave comes out tops for me – both in time and cost.

I think over the years since the 1980s fewer people invested in a microwave, thinking all they used it for was reheating food. Here are a number of energy- and time-saving tips. My microwave is 1000 watts and cooking times have been calculated accordingly – adjustments may be required for other machines.

FOOD AND PLATE WARMER

I think this is one of the superb advantages of the microwave. A plated meal can be reheated from cold quickly in a minute or two, whereas in a low oven it would quickly dry out, stick to the plate and, if kept warm too long, would lose its appeal – not to mention the energy cost. Clearly quick ready meals would not have such a large segment of the market were it not for the microwave.

Some machines have a dedicated plate-warmer button – mine doesn't. Simply squirt a spray of water over each plate, stack them up to four at a time and microwave on High for 30 seconds. Add a further 30 seconds if they are not warm enough after the first blast. Ensure plates don't have metal trims or patterns before putting them in the microwave.

MINUTE LEMON CURD

Made in a minute with minimal energy cost. I adore lemon curd and use it in many recipes – in cake fillings, Swiss rolls, added to cream to make a lemon pouring sauce, in tarts or just spread onto fresh bread. Delicious! A great way to use up leftover egg yolks. Traditionally this is made in a bain-marie or a bowl sitting over a pan of barely simmering water to prevent the lemon curd cooking quickly. Time, valuable energy and money are saved using this microwave method.

MAKES ABOUT 180G (6OZ)

You will need

small microwave-safe bowl
small whisk
fine grater
knife
chopping board
clean glass jar with lid

2 egg yolks
50g (1¾oz) sugar
35g (1¼oz) room-temperature butter, cut into dice
zest and juice of 1 lemon

Add the egg yolks, sugar and butter to the bowl and gently whisk. Finely grate the zest from the lemon straight into the bowl, then cut the lemon in half and squeeze out as much juice as possible.

|||||||||||||||||||||||||||||||||||||||||||||||||||||||||||||||||||||||||||||||||||||||||||||||||||||||||||

TIP: Before discarding the lemon halves, give your chopping board a quick clean and refresh by sprinkling over some table salt then giving it a rub over with the lemon half. Eliminate bacteria and neutralize onion-chopping odour!

|||||||||||||||||||||||||||||||||||||||||||||||||||||||||||||||||||||||||||||||||||||||||||||||||||||||||||

Give the mix a good stir, then pop into the microwave on High power for 20 seconds. Take it out, give it a quick whisk, then put it back in again for a further 20 seconds. After this second blast the butter should have melted, then it's back in for a final 20 seconds and the lemon curd should have thickened. If it still seems thin, this is due to the temperature of the ingredients being used – a further 20 seconds may be required to complete the thickening.

After a really good beating to emulsify, transfer the thick curd to a sterilized glass jar (see page 223), put on the lid then leave to cool at room temperature, where it will thicken further. Once cool, transfer to the fridge where it will keep for up to 4 weeks.

If you don't have a microwave, the lemon curd can be made in just the same way, but stirred over a gentle heat in a small saucepan until thickened.

STERILIZE JARS IN A JIFFY

Whether making lemon curd, jam or marmalade, rather than using the oven to sterilize jars, the microwave will do the job much quicker and cheaper.

After washing jars in hot soapy water, rinse then leave just a tablespoon of water in the base of each jar and pop into the microwave. Sterilize as many jars as will fit onto the microwave turntable – usually up to 8.

Microwave on High for 60 seconds or until you see that the water in the base of each jar is bubbling away, then turn off. If only one or two jars are being sterilized, the microwave time can be reduced to around 15 seconds. Discard any remaining water then fill with hot jams, pickles and preserves as per your recipe.

To sterilize metal lids, pop them into a small saucepan, cover in water then bring to a boil and simmer for 10 minutes to sterilize. Do not use lids that have become rusted or where the rubber seal has perished. Replacement lids can be purchased for some jars.

If you don't have a microwave the jars can be sterilized in a conventional oven. Place clean jars in a cold oven, turn on to 100°C/80°C fan/200°F/gas ¼ for 30 minutes. Turn off the oven, leave the jars in there until required. For Aga owners, clean jars can be placed in the bottom oven for 30 minutes.

NO-FAFF CRÈME PÂT!

Crème pâtissière is a delicious pastry cream that can be used in so many recipes, and it's a fantastic use for leftover egg yolks (and even frozen egg yolks, see page 152).

It can be used on its own to fill tarts and eclairs, whisked with double cream to make a cake filling, or whisked with evaporated milk to make a delicious budget no-churn ice cream.

However, I have read and used recipes that seem to over-complicate the making of it – creating several stages, fear and trepidation, plus excessive energy use and lots of unnecessary washing up.

Try this – all in a bowl or jug together – made in a couple of minutes in the microwave with minimal energy needed.

MAKES 400G (14OZ)

You will need

medium bowl or 1 litre (34fl oz) microwave-safe jug
plastic spatula, wooden fork or spoon

3 egg yolks
1 tsp vanilla extract
50g (1¾oz) sugar
25g (¾oz) cornflour
250ml (9fl oz) whole milk
15g (½oz) butter

Add the egg yolks to the bowl or jug (allow to defrost if using from frozen), then add the vanilla and sugar and stir until they become a coarse, thick paste – as thick as whipped double cream. Stir in the cornflour, and at this point the paste will be even thicker and stiff, yet smooth and without lumps.

Add the milk a little at a time – pouring all of the milk in at once will make mixing very difficult. Start with just 1–2 tablespoons, loosening the thick paste to a thinner batter slowly so the milk doesn't slosh around. Once all is incorporated, continue to add the milk to the now loosened mix – the batter will now be thin and without any lumps. Finally, add the knob of butter.

Microwave on High for 1 minute, take out, stir well, then pop it back into the microwave for another minute, after which time the crème pâtissière will be thickening. Put it back in for just another 10–20 seconds more and the custard will become very thick (consistency of softly whipped cream) and can be poured into tarts, or cover it with a plate to prevent a skin forming and leave to cool to use later. This will keep in the fridge for up to a week.

Even if you are not a keen baker or you have made the crème pâtissière to use up leftover egg yolks, you can turn this delicious thick custard quickly and easily into no-churn ice cream.

NO-CHURN 'BUDGET' CREAMY ICE CREAM

Ice cream is always a favourite, but after I examined the list of ingredients on any other than the very top-end tubs of ice cream, I decided to make my own. No ice-cream maker needed, just a plastic tub.

MAKES ABOUT 750ML (25¾FL OZ)

You will need

large mixing bowl
electric hand whisk
1 litre (34fl oz) plastic tub for freezing

300ml (10fl oz) double cream
400g (14oz) crème pâtissière, chilled
1 tsp vanilla extract

Whisk the double cream in a large mixing bowl until just beginning to thicken. Take 2–3 tablespoons of the thickening cream and add them to the bowl of chilled crème pâtissière and whisk together to loosen the crème pâtissière mix. Add more cream if necessary – the crème pât needs to be the same consistency as the cream.

Add the crème pât to the bowl of whipped cream and whisk briefly until the two come together. Transfer to the plastic tub and freeze for 5 hours or so until firm and able to be scooped.

Once the ice cream has been frozen beyond this time,

because it has no additives it will freeze hard, so take out of the freezer and transfer to the fridge for an hour before serving so you are able to spoon or scoop it.

|||||||||||||||||||||||||||||||||||||||||||||||||||||||||||||||||||||||||||||||||||||||||||||||||||||||||||||||||||||||||||||||||

TIP: Stir in 100g (3½oz) crushed frozen raspberries or blackberries for a fruited ripple ice cream. Add right at the end and stir through briefly, otherwise the ice cream will colour rather than ripple.

|||||||||||||||||||||||||||||||||||||||||||||||||||||||||||||||||||||||||||||||||||||||||||||||||||||||||||||||||||||||||||||||||

To make an ice cream with a softer scoop, add in 1–2 tablespoons of alcohol of choice – brandy is good (adult) option, or fruit cordial – neither will add a lot of flavour.

QUICK POACHED EGG BEFORE
YOUR TOAST HAS POPPED UP!

Here is a handy recipe that will have your egg made ahead of the toast, using less than one minute of microwave energy.

I make this a lot, especially when I need just a quick lunch for one or two people. The important point to note is the ambient temperature of the egg before cooking. An egg kept in the fridge or cold pantry in winter could be around 5°C, whereas an egg kept at room temperature in a warm kitchen in summer could be around 20°C – and obviously this will be important when calculating the perfect cooking time. I keep my eggs all year round at room temperature in the kitchen, which maintains a temperature of 18–19°C, and the cooking times are calculated accordingly. If your eggs are colder they need longer.

You will need

small deep bowl – a large cup can work well
slotted spoon
kitchen paper

1 fresh egg (better for poaching because the whites
    are firmer) weighing 55–65g (2–2¼oz) in the shell

Crack the egg into the bottom of the cup, then cover with water. I used 70ml (2¼fl oz) water in total, but be sure the water covers the egg completely and stands at least 1cm (½in) above the egg.

Microwave at 800 watts for 40 seconds, then stop and check your egg; the white should look as though it is firming up. Then microwave for a further 10, 15 or 20 seconds depending on egg size and personal preference. I like a runny yolk, which takes 50 seconds in total.

Remove from the bowl with a slotted spoon and drain on kitchen paper, then place on a slice of warm toast that's just popped out of the toaster.

SOFT- AND HARD-BOILED EGGS

If you have ever tried to cook eggs in the microwave, chances are you had an explosion with a huge mess to clean up – something that's not to be repeated. Table salt, however, can make all the difference. I add a good dose of salt to the water, which I once read will block some of the microwaves and ensure that the eggs cook evenly and gently, preventing any cracks in the shell or, at worst, explosions. I guess it must be a fact, as I have never had an egg explode on me using this method.

I have practised microwave egg cooking so many times to get it spot on. I had two of my granddaughters over one day and for lunch I said they could have boiled eggs and toast soldiers – an ideal opportunity to perfect microwave egg cooking, I thought. First attempt at two eggs (one each) – completely solid. 'This is not a dippy egg, Granny! But it's still nice . . .'

Second attempt – spot on. 'This one is just great, Granny – you don't need to make any more, we're full now!'

You will need

   small bowl
   measuring jug
   plate or saucer to cover bowl
   spoon
   plastic bottle and funnel
   slotted spoon

2 large eggs 55–65g (2–2¼oz) in weight, at room
  temperature
400ml (14fl oz) cold water
3 tsp table salt

Place the eggs into the bowl, pour over the water, then add the table salt and give it a quick stir. Cover with the plate or saucer and microwave at 800-watt power for 4 minutes. Don't be tempted to lift the plate or remove the bowl from the microwave, set the timer on your phone or keep an eye on the clock – 5 minutes for soft-boiled and 10 minutes for hard-boiled.

After the chosen standing time, remove the eggs using the slotted spoon and leave the cooking water to go completely cold – don't discard it. For hard-boiled eggs, transfer to a bowl of cold water to retain a good yolk colour (without a greenish band).

|||||||||||||||||||||||||||||||||||||||||||||||||||||||||||||||||||||||||||||||||||||||||||||||||||||||||||||||||||||||||

TIP: Bottle the heavily salted water and keep it for blood spill emergencies. You can use cold salt water to dab at carpet blood spills or as an overnight pre-soak solution for bloodstained garments. The salt water will dissolve any bloodstains before washing.

|||||||||||||||||||||||||||||||||||||||||||||||||||||||||||||||||||||||||||||||||||||||||||||||||||||||||||||||||||||||||

SCRAMBLED EGGS

When I purchased my first microwave back in the 1980s, quick scrambled eggs were a revelation. No burnt-on messy pan to wash up and scrambled eggs in a matter of minutes at a fraction of the cost of cooking them on the stove top or hob.

SERVES 2–3

You will need

microwave-safe bowl
wooden spoon or fork (or use metal, but only outside the microwave)

5 eggs
knob of butter
chopped chives or other fresh herbs (optional)
1 tbsp crème fraîche
salt and pepper, to taste

Crack the eggs into the bowl and beat together using the wooden (or metal) spoon or fork.

If the fork being used is wooden, leave it in the bowl, then put in the microwave for 30 seconds on High. Beat the eggs and place the bowl back in the microwave for another 30 seconds. Beat again, then return to the microwave for another 30 seconds, then take from the microwave, add the butter, salt and pepper, herbs, if using, and crème fraîche.

The eggs should look still quite liquid, but leave to stand in the microwave (where it is warm) for a further 30 seconds and they will firm up further to just the right consistency.

It is better to undercook the eggs; examine them after the standing time, then give a further 10- or 20-second blast if necessary rather than judge the eggs before the standing time, blast for longer and then to discover they are rubbery and overcooked.

DRIED CITRUS SLICES

Here is a quick and inexpensive way to dry citrus slices if you don't want to dry too many, you don't have a dehydrator and want to avoid the cost of using the oven. Drying in conventional appliances can take several hours – the microwave needs much less time and energy. I dried the slices from a large orange because I wanted to add them to my home-made natural Christmas wreath – but I wanted them quickly!

You will need

sharp knife
chopping board
kitchen paper
greaseproof paper

1 orange or lemon

Slice the orange or lemon then blot the slices with absorbent kitchen paper to mop up excess juice. Cut two rounds of greaseproof paper to match the size of the microwave turntable. Lay one down, then cover it with a layer of fruit slices and top with the other sheet. Microwave on High power for 30 seconds.

Remove the cover sheet, flip over the slices, then reduce the wattage to just 10 per cent power (100 watts in my oven), and set the timer for 30 minutes.

After the 30 minutes, remove the top paper, peel the drying

slices from the damp bottom paper and discard this sheet. Transfer the sticky slices onto the dry sheet that was used to cover them. Lay the dry paper with the fruit slices onto the turntable and microwave for a further 30 minutes, turning regularly, at 100 watts (10 per cent power) or until the slices are dry.

These are absolutely great for using on seasonal home-made natural decorations (wreaths, table centres, etc.), even though you may spot one or two dark spots on the slices where the microwave has gone overboard – you could always look upon them as additional decoration! To avoid this happening, though, keep a close eye on the slices and turn them regularly.

PASTA SALAD

Summer barbecues and buffet-style meals often include a bowl of cold pasta salad, and I love it. I add in a tin of tuna, diced cucumber and parsley with a touch of mayo, or simply halved cherry tomatoes, pesto, chopped peppers and basil. Rather than bringing a huge pan of water to the boil to cook the pasta, try this energy-efficient, quicker method that is great for cold pasta salads and for a quick bowl of hot pasta too.

You will need

large microwave-safe bowl with a lid, or plate to cover
colander

150g (5½oz) pasta (I often use fusilli, but any pasta shape)
300ml (10fl oz) cold water
drizzle of olive oil
salt and black pepper, to taste

||||||||||||||||||||||||||||||||||||||||||||||||||||||||||||||||||||||||||||||||||||||||||||||||||||||||||||||||||||||

TIP: For every weight of pasta, double the amount
of cold water and the water needs to just cover
the dried pasta.

||||||||||||||||||||||||||||||||||||||||||||||||||||||||||||||||||||||||||||||||||||||||||||||||||||||||||||||||||||||

Place the pasta and water into the bowl and microwave on High power for 3 minutes or until the water begins to boil and rises up the bowl. Reduce the power to 100 watts and cook for 15 minutes until the pasta is soft and cooked through.

Drain the pasta in the colander in the sink and rinse with cold running water. This will immediately cool the pasta and wash off excess starch that would cause it to stick together.

It can then be transferred to a bowl and stirred with a drizzle of oil and seasoning, then you can add your salad ingredients of choice.

||||||||||||||||||||||||||||||||||||||||||||||||||||||||||||||||||||||||||||||||||||||||||||||||||||||||||||||||||||||

TIP: Don't add salt to the cooking water, as salt slows down the cooking in the microwave. Always add the seasoning afterwards.

||||||||||||||||||||||||||||||||||||||||||||||||||||||||||||||||||||||||||||||||||||||||||||||||||||||||||||||||||||||

CRISPS

These are a fast, low-cost, low-energy, low-fat, low-salt snack. I love crisps, but I can find myself bingeing on them to such a degree that I can spoil my appetite. I now give myself a small bowl – reduced in salt and fat, no single-use plastic packaging and many fewer calories. I make a handy snack pot in the microwave. Roughly one potato weighing approximately 125g (4½oz) goes into each 25g (¾oz) pack of crisps – about 80 per cent of a potato is water. To make your own quickly, the thinner the slices, the quicker the drying time and the crisper the crisps. For flavour, try paprika, garlic granules, sea salt, powdered onion – have a look on your spice rack for inspiration. You can also do this with sliced carrot, parsnip, beetroot or any root vegetable – they are a great healthy snack.

SERVES 1

You will need

knife
chopping board
kitchen paper or clean tea towel
2 sheets of greaseproof paper

about 125g (4½oz) washed and dried potato, skin on
vegetable oil spray
salt and/or flavouring of choice (paprika, garlic granules,
    curry powder, etc.)

Cut the potato into slices as thinly as you can – when held up to the light the potato slice should be translucent. Using kitchen paper or a clean tea towel, mop up excess moisture from the potato slices and lay them in a single layer on grease-proof paper which has been cut to size to fit the microwave turntable. Spray over vegetable oil, cover with the second sheet of paper, then microwave on High for 3½ minutes.

Remove the paper to see that the potatoes are beginning to colour and cook. Turn them over, keeping them in a single layer, and continue to microwave in 30-second bursts until the potatoes are crisp. Remove the paper from the microwave, add salt and/or a dusting of flavour, if required, then transfer to a serving bowl.

TIP: To cut a circle of greaseproof paper to size, take a sheet of greaseproof paper just larger than the turntable, then fold it in half, half again, then half again, and keep going until your paper is shaped like a pointed arrow. Place the point towards the centre of the turntable and use scissors to cut the wide end in line with the outer edge. Open up the paper and you have a perfect-fitting circle of paper. Repeat for the second piece. I don't discard my 'crisp' paper, I save it to use next time for quick crisps.

5-MINUTE 'NEARLY FREE' VEGGIE STOCK

When making stews, soups and casseroles the recipe will usually call for stock. If you have planned ahead and made your own, brilliant; but if not and you need it now, rather than reaching for a proprietary and maybe heavily salted stock cube, make up this simple stock in minutes using your vegetable trimmings.

When preparing washed veggies for a recipe – potatoes, onions, carrots, celery, swede, turnips, peppers, peas, beans, parsley stalks, etc. – rather than transferring the peelings, skins, stalks or pods to the recycle or compost bin, pop them first into a large microwave-safe bowl.

Add a bay leaf, if you have one, then check out the amount of stock required for your recipe. Let us assume the recipe calls for 750ml (25fl oz) stock; add 750ml (25fl oz) water to the kettle, boil exactly the amount required, then pour over the veggie peelings. Cover then microwave on High for 5 minutes. The water will re-boil immediately and the stock can be used after the cooking time.

Strain through a colander directly into your stew or casserole when the recipe asks for it, then the cooked vegetable skins can be safely composted.

TIP: Keep a bag or box in the freezer to save veggie offcuts, then once you have a sizable amount, make a quick veggie stock.

FLEXI RECIPES

Energy costs are making us all think before turning on our appliances. Careful use of limited energy is of course welcome news for our planet's welfare, so even if we are fortunate enough to not have to consider cost, we need to have a conscience about the future of our planet and use energy wisely. No one is so rich as to not have to consider energy consumption.

I am trying more and more to make my recipes fit the situation. For example, if the oven is going on anyway I will make sure I fill it by batch cooking, baking or heating a pan of water for washing up, thereby utilizing and maximizing every single watt!

Other days, the oven may not go on at all, and at those times I may reheat a precooked meal in the microwave, use only the hob, maybe pull out a slow cooker or use my microwave to cook from scratch. I have tried to offer a series of options that will hopefully help you to adapt your favourite recipes too.

FLEXI MUSHROOM RISOTTO

You must try this. Whether you are vegetarian, vegan or, like me, a meat eater who is trying to eat more plant-based meals, then you are going to be impressed by this recipe. Super tasty, easy and, unlike other risotto recipes, I now cook mine from scratch in the oven along with a pudding, cake or tomorrow's casserole. No faff, it looks after itself. I also include hob, slow cooker and microwave cooking options to offer some flexibility.

SERVES 2–3

You will need

for oven: ovenproof frying pan or casserole with a well-fitting
    lid
for stove top or hob: large, roomy, deep-sided frying pan
for multicooker/slow cooker: use proprietary bowl
for microwave: deep non-metal dish or casserole with a lid

2 tbsp olive or rapeseed oil
1 small onion, finely chopped
1 tsp dried mixed herbs
250g (9oz) chestnut mushrooms, wiped and thinly sliced
1 leek, thinly sliced
50g (1¾oz) walnuts, finely chopped (optional)
1 clove of garlic, finely chopped, or ½ tsp garlic granules
750–800ml (25–27fl oz) hot mushroom or vegetable stock,
    or use a good-quality stock cube

200g (7oz) arborio or risotto rice

1 tsp fennel seeds, slightly crushed

½ tsp ground mace or 1 tsp ground nutmeg

pinch of salt and pepper

2 tbsp either chopped fresh sage, chives, thyme, parsley or wild
    garlic leaves, or a mix, or an additional tsp dried mixed herbs

1 cup frozen peas (optional)

2–3 tbsp single, double or soured cream (or non-dairy
    equivalent for a vegan dish)

grated vegetarian Parmesan or non-dairy alternative, to serve

Oven Method – about 50 minutes

Preheat the oven to 200°C/180°C fan/400°F/gas 6.

In a large ovenproof frying pan or casserole that has a well-fitting lid, add the oil then the chopped onion and dried mixed herbs, stir, then pop into the oven, uncovered, and cook for 10 minutes until the onion is softening but not browning.

Take the pan from the oven, then add the mushrooms, leek and nuts, plus the garlic. Give a good stir to combine then place the pan back into the oven, uncovered, for 15 minutes to fry.

While the pan is in the oven again, make up the stock using a quality stock pot or cube, if using, or even better use home-made (see page 240). The stock needs to be hot. Have weighed out and ready the rice, fennel seeds, mace or nutmeg, salt and pepper. If you are using peas, have them ready to add to the risotto after cooking.

Take the pan from the oven, add the rice, fennel seeds and spices, give it all a good stir, then pour over 750ml (25fl oz) of the hot stock (keep a little back in case it needs to be slackened off after the cooking time). Stir well, then add the lid and place the pan back into the oven and set your timer for 15 minutes. After 15 minutes take the pan from the oven, take the lid off and give it all a stir, then replace the lid and put back into the oven for another 15 minutes.

Test your risotto rice to make sure it is cooked through by trying a bit, then stir in the frozen peas, if using. I tend to add just a good handful of freshly chopped herbs. Stir through the cream or vegan alternative and check the seasoning, adding more salt and pepper if required and a final splash of stock if your risotto needs to be loosened slightly. A risotto needs to flow on the plate rather than sit in a solid lump, so if in doubt don't be afraid to add extra hot stock. A flowing risotto is better than a stuck one!

Serve on warm plates topped off with grated Parmesan or a non-dairy equivalent.

Stove Top/Hob Method – about 45 minutes

Heat the oil in a deep frying pan or saucepan, then on a medium heat fry the onion for about 10 minutes until starting to soften. Add the leeks, herbs, fennel seeds, nutmeg/mace, garlic, seasoning, mushrooms and walnuts and stir until the mushrooms and leeks are beginning to brown at the edges. Turn the heat down, add the rice, stir then pour in 700ml (24fl oz) of the hot stock. Stir well, turn down the heat to the lowest setting, then cover and simmer for 25–30 minutes, stirring from time to time (about every 5 minutes). The rice will absorb the stock as it cooks, so add the remainder if necessary towards the end of the cooking time. Add the peas, if using, stir through the cream, then add more stock if necessary to slacken the risotto. Heat through for 5 minutes then serve on warmed plates with grated Parmesan or a non-dairy equivalent.

Multicooker/Slow Cooker Method – about 1.5 hours

Begin by following the instructions for the Stove Top/Hob method above.

Those with a multicooker can start the onion frying in the bowl of the cooker, but for those using a traditional slow cooker you will need to start on the hob as above, before transferring all the ingredients to the preheated slow cooker.

Turn on the slow cooker when starting to fry the onions on the hob/stove top. Transfer the onions, leek, herbs, fennel seeds, nutmeg/mace, garlic, seasonings, mushrooms and walnuts into the slow cooker after frying. Add the rice and all of the stock. Stir, cover and slow-cook on High for 1.5 hours, stirring halfway through (though if you want to go out, it'll be fine). Stir through the peas, cream and/or freshly chopped herbs just before serving, and top with the cheese or vegan equivalent.

Microwave Method – about 45 minutes

In a deep, non-metal dish or casserole with a lid (mine is Pyrex) place the oil and the onions and cook on High for 2 minutes. Stir, then add the leeks and cook for a further 1 minute. Add in the herbs, fennel seeds, nutmeg/mace, garlic, seasonings, mushrooms, walnuts, rice and stock, give a good stir and microwave on High for 5 minutes or until you see that the mix is boiling.

Stir well then turn down to 10 per cent power or 100 watts and microwave for 30–40 minutes, covered, stirring halfway through. Microwaves differ, so check after 30 minutes' cooking time. My rice was cooked just right, but you may need to taste and check your rice to make sure it is cooked through.

If it still feels hard it will need a further 10 minutes in the microwave.

When cooked, stir well, add the peas if using, plus more hot stock/water if necessary. Check the seasoning and stir in the cream. Leave to stand for 2–3 minutes then serve onto hot plates with the Parmesan cheese and freshly chopped herbs.

FLEXI VEGGIE STEW WITH
A CHEEKY NO-COOK DESSERT
ON THE SIDE

This wholesome, hearty stew is a great winter warmer for those wanting to cut down their meat intake, or for those wanting a gluten-free, dairy-free or low-fat diet, and will tick the boxes for vegetarians and vegans too. This stew can be cooked on the hob, in the oven, in the Aga, in a slow cooker or a pressure cooker. I reserve the liquid from the tin of chickpeas (aquafaba) which can be whipped up to serve a light and delicious budget chocolate mousse for four or five people for afters.

SERVES 4–5

You will need

for oven/Aga cooking: ovenproof casserole with a well-fitting lid
for stove top or hob cooking: ovenproof casserole pan with
    a lid
for slow cooker/pressure cooker: frying pan and proprietary
    bowl

chopping board
knife
bowl for soaking pulses
sieve for straining
large mixing bowl
hand-held electric whisk

microwave-safe bowl
small bowls or serving glasses

1–2 tbsp vegetable oil
2 onions, finely chopped
2–3 cloves of garlic, chopped
1 celery stick, chopped
1 tbsp dried mixed herbs (or use 2 tbsp chopped fresh
    herbs)
800g (1lb 12oz) fresh mixed winter vegetables (peeled
    weight of carrots, celeriac, sweet potato, leeks, parsnips,
    potatoes), chopped into 2cm (¾in) dice
½ tsp chilli powder, 1 tsp hot chilli sauce or 1 medium fresh
    chilli (green or red), finely chopped
100g (3½oz) lentils, beans and/or pulses (choose Puy,
    red or green lentils, yellow or green split peas, dried
    beans), pre-soaked in 300ml (10fl oz) cold water for
    12 hours
1 x 400g (14oz) tin chickpeas in water
1 x 400g (14oz) tin chopped tomatoes or 400ml (14fl oz)
    passata
800ml (27fl oz) hot vegetable stock from a cube or home-
    made (see page 240)
1 cup frozen peas
salt and pepper, to taste

FOR THE CHOCOLATE MOUSSE
about 180ml (6½ fl oz) strained water from chickpeas
    (aquafaba)
½ tsp cream of tartar

45g (1½oz) icing sugar
100g (3½oz) dark chocolate (or milk, white or vegan)
1 tsp vanilla extract
sugar sprinkles or chopped fresh raspberries, to decorate

To make the stew, in a large saucepan, the bowl of a multi-cooker, pressure cooker, ovenproof casserole or a large frying pan (if continuing the cooking in a slow cooker), heat the oil then fry the onions and garlic for 5–10 minutes over a low heat until starting to soften. Stir in the celery and herbs, a hefty pinch of salt and pepper and cook a few minutes, then add the prepared veggies.

Turn the heat up to high and fry the vegetables until they are just starting to colour at the edges. Stir regularly so that they don't burn. The light caramelization of the veg helps to bring out their flavours. To each of the below methods, when you add the strained chickpeas – make sure to reserve the aquafaba (chickpea water) in a separate bowl for the dessert.

To oven cook
Add the rest of the ingredients and give them a good stir. Cover the casserole with a well-fitting lid and transfer to the oven preheated to 200°C/180°C fan/400°F/gas 6 for about an hour or until the vegetables are tender and the stew has thickened.

In the slow cooker
After first frying the onions and browning the veggies in a frying pan on the hob, transfer the frying pan contents to the bowl of a preheated slow cooker (preheat for half an hour), then add the rest of the ingredients, stir well, then cook for

5–6 hours or until the vegetables are tender and the stew has thickened.

In the pressure cooker
After frying the onions and vegetables in the pan of the pressure cooker, add the stock and the rest of the ingredients, then Pressure cook on High for 20 minutes.

For hob/stove top cooking
After frying the onions and browning the vegetables, add the stock and rest of the ingredients. Bring to the boil then reduce to a simmer, cover and cook for 40–50 minutes or until the vegetables are tender.

For Aga cooking
Bring to the boil on the hot plate, cover, then transfer to the low simmering oven for 2–3 hours or until the vegetables are tender and the stew is thickened.

When ready to serve, taste the stew and adjust the seasoning, if necessary, then stir through the peas and serve in warmed bowls.

To make the chocolate mousse, pour the reserved water from the chickpeas into a large mixing bowl, add the cream of tartar and whisk up with a hand-held electric whisk until the mix is light, white and standing in soft peaks. Aquafaba behaves exactly like egg white and is a favourite with vegans. Add the vanilla and then the icing sugar in two parts, whisking well between each addition.

In a microwave-safe bowl, break up the chocolate into small

pieces then microwave on High in two 30-second bursts until it is fully melted. Take a spoonful of the whipped mixture and stir it into the chocolate to loosen it, then pour the whole lot into the mixing bowl and stir to combine.

Pour the chocolate mix between four or five small bowls or serving glasses, banging them down on the work surface to smooth and release any air pockets. Add a few sugar sprinkles or chopped fresh raspberries to decorate, then place in the fridge for an hour or two until the mousse fully sets.

FLEXI CHOCOLATE FUDGE SLICE

This has to be the simplest yet deliciously moist **flexi chocolate** tray-bake recipe. Made in minutes in the microwave or it can be baked in the oven when it goes on for something else.

MAKES 12 PIECES

You will need

for oven baking: 18cm (7in) square cake tin – loose-
    bottomed if you have it
for microwave: 18cm (7in) square or 20cm (8in) round
    non-metallic dish or silicone mould
greaseproof paper
medium mixing bowl
digital weighing scales
hand-held electric whisk
spatula or wooden spoon
teaspoon
microwave-safe jug, bowl or small saucepan of water
cooling rack

lining paste (see page 16), optional
120g (4½oz) soft butter or margarine
1 tsp vanilla extract
100g (3½oz) sugar
120g (4½oz) self-raising flour
25g (¾oz) cocoa powder

80ml (2½fl oz) milk

2 eggs

FOR THE FUDGE TOPPING

100g (3½oz) dark chocolate

30g (1oz) butter

25ml (¾fl oz) boiling water

sugar sprinkles, to decorate

For oven baking

Prepare the tin by greasing it with butter or brushing with lining paste, then line the base with a square of greaseproof paper.

To mix the cake simply place the bowl onto the scales, set to zero, then weigh all of the ingredients into the bowl, finishing with the eggs. Whisk on a slow speed until the batter is thick, dark and smooth.

Transfer to the prepared tin and smooth to the sides using the back of a teaspoon. This batter will happily sit in the fridge for 2–3 hours until the oven goes on for something else. Bake at 180°C/160°C fan/350°F/gas 4 for 18–20 minutes. When baked through the cake will be slightly risen, just beginning to crack, and feel firm to the touch when a finger is placed in the centre. If in doubt, touch the outside edge of the cake to know what the fully baked sponge feels like (the outside bakes first) then use the same finger to feel the centre. If it feels the same the cake is baked successfully. If the centre feels softer, with no resistance to the finger, it needs another 10 minutes or so before checking again. Don't take the cake from the oven to do this, try to do it while the cake is still in the heat so that you don't get a sudden dip if the batter isn't cooked through.

While the cake is baking, prepare the fudge topping. Break the chocolate into small pieces, pop into the microwave-safe jug, add the butter, cut into cubes, then pour over the boiling water. Stir with a wooden spoon until smooth and glossy. If the chocolate doesn't quite melt, pop it into the microwave for just 15–20 seconds to ensure it is fully melted.

Place the baked cake onto a cooling rack, allow to cool for 5–10 minutes in the tin, or until the tin is cool enough to handle, then pour over the thick warm fudge topping. Tilt the tin from side to side until the fudge covers the whole surface. Scatter over a few sprinkles for decoration and leave to cool completely.

Remove from the tin and onto a board and pop into the freezer for just 10–15 minutes. If you have used a loose-bottomed tin, freeze it with the base still intact. After a quick cold blast the cake will have firmed up sufficiently so that you can handle it easily without causing any damage or leaving fingerprints in the topping.

You can stand the cake on its side, peel off the greaseproof base paper, then lay it flat to cut into 12 neat fingers without crumbs or cracks in the chocolate.

TIP: This cake freezes well too. Open-freeze the cake slices on a tray lined with greaseproof paper, and once frozen pack into a box. When you fancy a slice of cake, take it out of the freezer and leave uncovered on a plate – it'll be thawed and good to eat in around an hour.

To microwave

Mix all of the ingredients as for the oven method. Transfer to the prepared microwave-safe dish or silicone mould. Bake on High for just 3 minutes at 1000 watts or 4 minutes at 800 watts. Check after the time to ensure the centre of the cake is firm – if not, add a further 30 seconds. Leave to stand for 2 minutes, then to cool for a further 5 minutes, then pour over the warm fudge topping, per the instructions given for the oven method.

FLEXI RICE PUDDING

Many people love a good rice pudding. It is nostalgic, comforting, cheap and will certainly put to good use any milk that is fast approaching its expiry date. This recipe will cook perfectly in the oven (for those that like the caramel golden skin), on the hob, in a slow cooker and even in the microwave. The recipe can be adapted for vegans, is naturally gluten free and freezes well too.

SERVES 6-8

You will need

2 litre (67fl oz) casserole or ovenproof dish
wooden spoon
large saucepan
large microwave-safe bowl or lidded Pyrex-type casserole

DAIRY RECIPE
30g (1oz) butter, for greasing
150g (5oz) pudding rice or risotto rice (washed in cold
    water in a sieve and left to drain)
50g (1¾oz) sugar
1 litre (34fl oz) whole milk
1 tsp vanilla extract
1 tsp grated nutmeg, plus extra
400ml (14fl oz) tin of evaporated milk

VEGAN RECIPE

- 150g (5oz) pudding or short grain rice (washed in cold
  water in a sieve and left to drain)
- 50g (1¾oz) sugar
- 1 litre (34fl oz) almond milk (or other dairy-free
  option)
- 1 tsp vanilla extract
- 1–2 tsp grated nutmeg
- 200g (7oz) block cream coconut (or 400g/14oz tin of
  coconut milk and omit the 200ml/7fl oz water)
- 200ml (7fl oz) water

For oven baking

Grease the casserole or ovenproof dish with butter then add all of the remaining ingredients. Give it a stir then pop into the oven preheated to 150°C/130°C fan/300°F/gas 2. The rice pudding can be stirred halfway through the cooking and an extra grating of nutmeg added. Bake for 2–2½ hours or until the pudding wobbles ever so slightly when shaken – no runny milk, the rice is soft, cooked through, and the pudding is thick with a dark baked skin.

||||||||||||||||||||||||||||||||||||||||||||||||||||||||||||||||||||||||||||||||||||||||||||||||||||||

TIP: Rub the base of your pan with butter to help avoid the milk burning on the bottom. Better still, a non-stick pan will work well as long as you don't have your heat too high.

||||||||||||||||||||||||||||||||||||||||||||||||||||||||||||||||||||||||||||||||||||||||||||||||||||||

For stove top/hob cooking

Place all the ingredients in a large saucepan, then set over a low heat and stir well until the butter (and coconut milk for the vegan version) and sugar have dissolved: Bring to a very gentle simmer then turn to the lowest setting and allow it to just tick over, stirring from time to time so that it doesn't burn on the bottom and so that the rice doesn't clump together. Try to stir about every 5 minutes or so.

Allow to cook for about 30 minutes, stirring regularly until the rice is *al dente* and almost cooked through. Take from the heat, place a lid on and leave to cool.

When cool the rice should be thick, creamy and completely tender. Give it a good stir and a taste. To serve, either reheat in the pan or microwave in individual bowls.

IIIIIIIIIIIIIIIIIIIIIIIIIIIIIIIIIIIIIIIIIIIIIIIIIIIIIIIIIIIIIIIIIIIIIIIIIIIIIIIIIIIIIIIIIIIIIIIIIIIIIIIIIIIIIIIIIIIIII

TIP: If you cook by gas and find it difficult to get a very gentle heat, an upturned baking tin over the flame will diffuse the heat, giving you just sufficient to cook the rice pudding.

IIIIIIIIIIIIIIIIIIIIIIIIIIIIIIIIIIIIIIIIIIIIIIIIIIIIIIIIIIIIIIIIIIIIIIIIIIIIIIIIIIIIIIIIIIIIIIIIIIIIIIIIIIIIIIIIIIIIII

To microwave

Reduce your fuel costs and make this family-friendly pudding in the microwave. My microwave is 1000 watts, so adjust cooking times accordingly depending on the wattage of your machine.

Add all of the ingredients to the large microwave-safe bowl or lidded Pyrex-type casserole, stir, cover, then microwave on

High for 13–15 minutes, stirring halfway through, until the milk starts to boil. Stir once more then turn the power down to just 10 per cent (100 watts) and cook for a further 40 minutes. At the end of the cooking time, leave to stand for 20 minutes. I tend to then leave mine to completely cool and thicken further and reheat it the next day. If you prefer to eat it at once and the pudding isn't thick enough for you, continue to cook in 1- to 2-minute blasts until the consistency is as you like it. No need to butter the cooking dish as the microwave rice pudding doesn't stick.

This rice pudding freezes well too – freezing in individual portions is handy, and to defrost I take it out of the freezer the night before to thaw overnight in the fridge, if I remember. If I forget, I take it out the next morning to thaw at room temperature for serving in the evening.

FLEXI SHORTBREAD

When it comes to baking, how do I choose between the oven and microwave? While a cake will rise up in seconds in the microwave, what is lacking is that oven-baked golden finish, so I prefer to either bake less often or batch-bake in the oven, because I want my baking to look good. However, there are certain baked recipes that lend themselves perfectly to microwave cooking and one that adapts beautifully is shortbread.

Shortbread doesn't need to be browned and the wonderful advantage of microwave shortbread is the reduction in energy consumption. I bake my shortbread in the oven for about an hour at a low temperature so that it doesn't colour, whereas just over ten minutes in the microwave and it's done!

I have baked this many times and tried to compare the two. When I think that maybe the oven-baked version has a very slight advantage in the finished bake, I am then easily swayed when I realize the microwave bake has taken a few minutes compared to an hour, and smugly only pennies' worth of energy and no baking tin to wash up.

MAKES 12 SLICES

You will need

for microwave: greaseproof paper
pencil
scissors
23cm (9in) plate, cake tin or flan ring

for oven baking: metal tablespoon or angled palette knife
small glass tumbler
fork
knife
23cm (9in) loose-bottomed fluted flan tin

mixing bowl
electric hand whisk, spatula or wooden spoon
rolling pin
fork and sharp-bladed knife
round-bladed knife

230g (8oz) room-temperature butter (not spread or
    margarine)
1 tsp vanilla extract
100g (3½oz) sugar
230g (8oz) plain flour (or use a mix of flours – white, bread
    flour, and a little wholemeal for a deeper taste and texture)
100g (3½oz) fine polenta, semolina or ground rice (I particularly
    like to use polenta because it is fine and the natural golden
    colour gives a 'baked and golden' finish to the shortbread)
1–2 tbsp caster sugar, for dusting

||||||||||||||||||||||||||||||||||||||||||||||||||||||||||||||||||||||||||||||||||||||||||||||||||||||||||||

TIP: If you can't find ground rice in the shops,
blitz uncooked rice to a fine powder in a food
processor or coffee grinder

||||||||||||||||||||||||||||||||||||||||||||||||||||||||||||||||||||||||||||||||||||||||||||||||||||||||||||

To microwave

Take the turntable from the microwave, place on top of a sheet of greaseproof paper, draw around it, then cut out the circle of greaseproof paper. Draw a pencil line around a 23cm (9in) plate, cake tin or flan ring centred onto the paper then flip it over so that the pencil line is underneath but can still be seen. This will act as a guide as there is no baking tin involved in this microwave method.

Cream together the butter, vanilla and sugar in a mixing bowl using the electric hand whisk, wooden spoon or spatula. Add in the flour and polenta, semolina or ground rice. I prefer to do this in small quantities because the dough needs to be very thick, and if added all in one go it can become difficult to manage. When the dough becomes thick I ditch the mixer, which begins to clog up anyway, and knead using my hands.

As the dough is very dry, you may feel all of the flour will never mix in, but it will and is even easier if your hands are warm and you have dampened them with water, then the job is done in half the time. It's much quicker by hand than trying to use utensils. Once the dough has formed into a ball, it is ready to transfer to the paper on the microwave turntable.

Press the dough down using your hands, then using the rolling pin, roll out the dough on the greaseproof paper already on the microwave turntable until it roughly fills the shape of the pencil line. Use the heels of your hands to mould the dough into a rough circle, staying within the pencil guideline.

Use the point of the knife to score 12 pieces. I score in half, then into quarters, then divide each quarter into three. Within each of the 12 pieces use the prongs of the fork to make a neat traditional shortbread pattern of your choice.

If the dough feels very soft, pop it into the fridge for 10 minutes to firm up as it will make cooking more successful.

Know the power wattage of your microwave machine. Mine is 1000 watts so I adjust down to 800 watts when ready to cook. Replace the turntable covered with the prepared shortbread dough and microwave on High for 9 minutes. Stop the microwave every 3 minutes and check the shortbread. It is quite interesting to watch the process; my machine cooks from the outside inwards so the outside edge appears to rise slightly as it cooks first. I have had followers tell me theirs cooked from the inside outwards, so just remember to keep an eagle eye! Use the round-bladed knife to gently push the shortbread back into its circle shape if it appears to be going off course slightly.

The dough doesn't look very promising at first and in my machine the centre was the last to cook – or should I say, 'dry out'. It stayed waxy looking until the 9 minutes was up.

I have also made this shortbread in a more modern microwave without a turntable. I still placed the dough on a circle of greaseproof paper and set onto a flat round plate. I figured this machine would be much more efficient than the one I was used to so turned the wattage down to just 600w. It behaved quite differently, puffing up here and there but after an extended cooking time of 12 minutes (checking every 3 minutes as before) the shortbread looked even at which time I took it out, redefined the lines etc, finished for another 90 seconds and it was perfect. It really is about understanding your own appliance and adjusting the wattage if necessary.

When the whole of the shortbread looks the same, remove

from the microwave, redefine the score lines and holes, then pop back in for a further 1 minute – still at 800 watts.

Take from the microwave, dust over with the caster sugar while still hot and soft, then leave to cool completely, after which time the slices can be cut through completely. The shortbread will be firm and crisp.

I find there is absolutely no difference in appearance or taste whether baked in the oven or microwave, though as microwave ovens vary cooking temperatures may differ.

For oven baking

small glass tumbler
fork
knife

Follow the recipe and method for the microwave shortbread, but instead press the dough into the lightly greased 23cm (9in) tin using your hands and press out to the edges with your fingers. Then smooth the dough as best you can using the back of a tablespoon or angled palette knife. Once the whole of the tin has a layer of dough, use a small glass tumbler to help smooth and flatten the surface completely.

Use the handle end of the fork to press the dough into the fluted edge around the outside of the shortbread, then use the knife to score 12 even-sized pieces. I score into quarters then score each quarter into three. Use the prongs of the fork to add shortbread-style patterns to each portion then bake in a low oven at 150°C/130°C fan/300°F/gas 2 for 55–60 minutes.

Take from the oven, allow to cool for 5 minutes in the tin, then redefine the score lines using a sharp knife. Dust over with caster sugar while warm then leave to cool completely in the tin.

Once cold, remove from the tin, cut along the score lines and enjoy.

The shortbread will keep in an airtight tin for up to 10 days.

CELEBRATIONS
AND GIFTS

B irthdays, Christmas, Easter, weddings, christenings – all of these celebrations can put pressure on the stretched monthly budget. How many of us have a heavy heart when three family birthdays fall in one month, or feel the pressure of Christmas present buying or an exciting wedding on the horizon, with all the added finery of favours, flowers, printing and stationery – not to mention the cake!

You know how I love a story . . . One Christmas I decided rather than having my usual frantic shopping spree, credit card in pocket to go out and buy a range of gifts for the adults in the family, I would instead put together a home-made gift hamper. This wasn't at the time so much about not wanting to spend money, I just didn't know what to buy people.

Of course, there are ready-made gift sets displayed in all of the shops, ranging from cosmetics to garden tools to baking sets. In fact, there is probably a gift set to fit every hobby and lifestyle, yet they all have one thing in common – they all contain minute tubes and jars that have often been craftily bulked out with lots of unnecessary packaging. Both the buyer and recipient believe they have a large gift when in fact the volume is simply lots of glossy cardboard and plastic film – often not suitable for recycling, either.

Then there are the gadgets – some fun, some practical – but

so often plastic, and because in the past I hadn't given enough thought to the purchase at the outset, it would then probably not be valued at all by the recipient, and would be thrown to the back of a drawer or cupboard for a while, to finally end its days in landfill. There are the edible gifts, of course. I always consider these a better idea, but again they can include excess packaging and so often excess salt and sugar too. No wonder that when you examine the best-before date it may be in excess of 12 months hence!

My Christmas hampers, on the other hand, were a huge hit! From the wrapping to the contents, to the labelling and the containers – everything was home-made, recycled or reused. I tried to make sure I kept costs down and had my 'eco-friendly' hat on the whole time. I can always find time to do things I want to do – the hampers used my time but I would rather spend it creating individual gifts than trudging around the shops glumly seeking inspiration. Do you know the best bit? These hampers were remembered and are still mentioned from time to time. Can I remember a shop-bought gift I received a couple of Christmases ago? Probably not, though I can remember that my sister-in-law gifted me hyacinths in a bowl that she planted herself some ten years ago that still pop up in the garden every spring.

HAMPER

I thought I would add here a little note about what to put all of your handmade goodies into. We all recognize the shop-bought hamper basket, overflowing with items of interest then glossed up with cellophane, ribbons and bows. When the festivities have ended, the basket may be tossed into a shed as it is too good to throw away. You realize it can be upcycled for something, but you haven't decided what yet. When I looked I had several such containers – little baskets that had contained flowers, one had been the presentation vessel for a collection of cheese and biscuits, and one had housed a mini selection of chutneys.

When constructing my hampers, I considered the 'end of life' of the container and decided instead to choose something practical. One year I put everything together in a cool box that could be reused, and more recently everything went into a large, traditional 'pancheon' glazed mixing bowl. Shredded packaging paper in the base, the gifts arranged decoratively on top, then all tied off with a sheet of eco-friendly clear gift wrap – gorgeous! Any recycled container can be used – a sturdy cardboard box is fine!

AWARD-WINNING MARMALADE

I am not one to brag (though I will anyway), but this recipe was awarded Silver in the Seville 'Full Fruit' World Marmalade Awards back in 2021, and even though I say it myself, once you've tasted your own home-made, then shop-bought just doesn't hit the spot.

Making your own is a fraction of the cost of the 'best' bought marmalade, even after factoring in the energy cost. Recycle your jars and make enough for yourself, then why not make an extra batch to add into a hamper or offer as an Easter gift?

Seville oranges have a very short season – only about six weeks during January and early February – and what I love about marmalade is there is no waste, as every scrap of orange is used to make the recipe. It's naturally gluten free, vegetarian and vegan too!

Allow four hours for marmalade-making. The first time I made it I started early evening and then couldn't go to bed because I was waiting for it to reach a set! The house was filled with a lovely fresh orange fragrance that is much better enjoyed during the day than last thing at night!

MAKES APPROXIMATELY 6 X 450G (1LB) JARS

You will need

citrus press or juicer attachment on a food processor
teaspoon
a brand-new cotton dishcloth (the double thickness type),

cut open at one end to give a loosely woven pocket of
cloth, is the cheapest option; or buy a 30cm (12in)
square piece of muslin or cheesecloth

cotton string (not the coloured plastic type)

knife

chopping board

a very large, 8 litre (17 pint) casserole or preserving pan

2 tea plates or saucers

wooden spoon

large bowl for the pips

rubber gloves

sugar thermometer (optional)

Pyrex jug

6 x 450g (1lb) glass jars with screw tops

1kg (2lb 4oz) Seville oranges

1 large or 2 small lemons

2 litres (3½ pints) water

2kg (4lb 8oz) granulated sugar

Start by juicing the fruits. I have a juice attachment on my
food processor, but otherwise, squeeze out as much juice as
possible and put it into the pan containing the water. Next,
with the pointed end of a teaspoon, scrape out the layer of
white pith attached to the orange skin along with the pips
from the fruit, plus the dried buds from the ends of the fruit
peels, and place these into the pocket of the dishcloth. It is
important to keep and use these valuable scraps because they
contain the pectin which will go on to set the marmalade.

Once the bag of scraps has been collected, secure it with
string and tie onto the handle of the pan, allowing it to sit in

the water. Next, take all the orange and lemon fruit shells and cut into thin strips. This can seem tiresome but the thinner the strips, the lovelier the marmalade will be. I have a 100-year-old Spong Marmalade Slicer, which I would love to boast is an heirloom but was in fact a sneaky eBay purchase, and even though it is a bit rough and ready – and I certainly wouldn't want to get my finger stuck in it – it slices the finest shreds. I have attempted shredding using a food processor one year, then a mandoline another year to try to speed up the slicing, but to be honest by the time you've got the kit out, fiddled, unclogged then washed up the various component parts – being left with chunks rather than shreds – hand-slicing ends up being quicker and the finished marmalade more beautiful. Put your favourite music on and enjoy the colour and perfume from these fabulous fruits.

Transfer the fruit strips into the pan with the water and juice, then set over a high heat, bring to the boil, then turn the heat down and simmer for 2 hours – yes, 2 hours – which may seem an excessive use of energy, but for me it is well worth the cost because of the yield, total final cost saving and, most importantly, the taste!

Ensure the marmalade simmers only very gently. Take a look in the pan – just quiet bubbles here and there – the heat should be at its lowest setting. Too fast and the water will evaporate off and the resultant marmalade will be too thick. At the end of the cooking time the strips of peel are tender and soft and will easily break using a wooden spoon.

During this long simmering time, put the sugar in a warm place. I have placed an unopened bag on a radiator or poured it into a large mixing bowl and placed it by the fire, or popped into a low oven at 100°C/80°C fan/200°F/gas ¼ to warm it through for half an hour. This will prevent the marmalade being cooled down too much when the sugar is added.

After the 2 hours' cooking time, the first thing to do is remove the bag of pith and pips. Place in a bowl and allow to cool down. I leave the bag for 15–20 minutes (often out in the cold air outside), after which time the bag can be handled wearing rubber gloves. I carefully squeeze the bag over the bowl, massaging and pushing out the lovely gooey pectin. Collect as much as you can, then once you feel you've squeezed every last gloop, set the bag to one side and transfer the thick gloopy pectin into the hot pan containing the cooked peel.

Once cooled, I transfer the bag's contents to the compost heap, wash the dishcloth, dry it and store it with my marmalade slicer until next year. I used to use a new dishcloth for every marmalade making session – not any more!

Carefully add the now-warmed sugar to the pan and stir over a gentle heat until completely dissolved. You will know when this has happened because as you stir with a wooden spoon the feel will go from gritty to smooth, and when taking the spoon out of the pan the back of the spoon will go from having speckles of undissolved sugar to being completely shiny and clear.

At this point I then place the 2 tea plates or saucers in the freezer and my clean jars into the warm oven that had the sugar – this will both heat and sterilize them (see page 223 for a quicker, low-energy method to sterilize your jars). To sterilize previously used lids, wash, pop into a small saucepan and boil for 10 minutes; then I leave them in the water until ready to use.

Bring the oranges and sugar up to a fast boil and keep it there for about 20 minutes – stir from time to time with a wooden spoon to prevent any sticking or burning. If you have a sugar thermometer, the marmalade has reached its correct temperature at 104°C (219°F), though I prefer to check using the saucer method. Take one of the tea plates/saucers from the freezer and put a spoonful of the marmalade onto it. Pop it into the fridge for a couple of minutes, then remove the plate and push the cooled liquid from one end with your finger. If the finger leaves a trail or the marmalade has formed a skin which crinkles when pushed, the marmalade is done. If, on the other hand, the liquid backfills when your finger pushes through and no skin is present, then give it another 10 minutes' boiling and repeat the process using the other clean chilled plate.

When the marmalade is done, take it off the heat, give it a thorough stir, then leave to stand for 20 minutes. This is important because as the marmalade cools it will start to thicken, holding in place the orange shreds. If it is poured into jars straight away the peel will float to the top, and though it will still taste amazing, it'll not look as gorgeous when gifted!

Take the warm jars from the oven (or microwave) and pour from the pan to the jar – I use a Pyrex jug for this. Place the tops on while still hot and label when cold.

This marmalade has a shelf life of at least two years, so it's a fantastic gift!

CHRISTMAS CAKE

My Christmas cake recipe I have always considered to be budget-friendly and it is extremely easy to make. It has been on the go for many years in my house; I don't mess with it, I keep the recipe the same and I know many followers use it year after year too.

When it comes to edible Christmas gifts, the shops are full of them – packs of chocolates, preserves, sweets, mince pies and Christmas cakes!

A home-made mini Christmas cake is a fantastic hamper filler, teacher gift, edible treat for someone that lives alone and the perfect pressie for the person who is impossible to buy for. The problem with a 7½cm (3in) mini cake such as this is that while the cost of the ingredients can be minimal, the price of the baking tin can be significant.

However, this is one of my favourite upcycles! A 200g (7oz) baked bean tin is the perfect size and baking vessel for a small Christmas cake, so I start to save them up well before my Christmas cake baking time, usually in October/November, though they can be made right up to Christmas if necessary. After using the contents of the can, remove the label along with the base using a tin opener, then carefully wash and dry the metal sleeve. Remember, although one end of the tin will be blunt and quite harmless, the opposite end once cut will have a very sharp edge. I keep the sharp end uppermost on the baking tray, then I always have my eye on it.

MAKES 9 INDIVIDUAL CAKES, OR A 23CM (9IN) ROUND OR
20CM (8IN) SQUARE CAKE

You will need

large bowl to soak the fruit
fine grater
plate, to cover
9 200g-size bean tins, or a 23cm (9in) round, or 20cm
    (8in) square deep cake tin
baking sheet
greaseproof paper
large mixing bowl
electric hand whisk or table-top mixer if you have one
measuring jug
fork
small bowl for flour and spices
spatula or large metal spoon
ice cream scoop or tablespoon

1kg (2lb 4oz) mixed dried fruit and peel
100g (3½oz) glacé cherries (cut into thirds)
finely grated zest and juice of 1 orange and 1 lemon
4 tbsp Cointreau, brandy, sherry (or 4 tbsp lemon juice/
    orange juice or cold tea)
spray oil, for greasing
250g (9oz) salted butter
250g (9oz) dark brown soft sugar
1 tbsp golden syrup (bought or home-made, see page 196)
    or black treacle
5 eggs

250g (9oz) plain flour
1 tsp ground mace (or 2 tsp ground nutmeg)
1 tsp mixed spice
1 tsp ground ginger
½ tsp ground cinnamon

Start the night before. Place the mixed fruits, cherries, fruit zests and juice in the large bowl and add the Cointreau or non-alcoholic liquid, stir and cover with a plate then leave until the next morning – or for several days in a cool place if you are busy.

On the day of baking, set the 9 bean tins on a large baking sheet, or prepare the cake tin if making one large cake. For all tins, line each on the base and inside with a collar of grease-proof paper, secure with a spray of oil and the tins are ready for use. Don't be worried that the tins have no bottom – the Christmas cake batter is very thick and will not leak.

When ready to mix, take the large mixing bowl (or the bowl of a table-top mixer) and cream together the butter and brown sugar until pale, light and fluffy using the electric hand whisk or paddle attachment of the table-top mixer.

Add the syrup or treacle and continue to mix. Break the eggs into the measuring jug and beat to combine using a fork, then gradually add the beaten egg a little at a time along with a teaspoon of flour, mixing well between each addition. This helps to prevent the mixture from curdling.

As a guide, add a quarter of the egg mix and a teaspoon of flour, mix, then repeat until all of the egg is incorporated and the batter is smooth. If the batter looks curdled at this stage – not smooth, slightly grainy and with an appearance of scram-bled egg – then turn up the speed of the machine or whisk and beat well until smooth. A curdled batter is not the end of the world but can impede the rise, so a good beating will sort it out before the flour is added.

When all the egg has been incorporated, the batter is happy and behaving itself then you're ready to add the rest of the flour. First sift the flour with the spices in a separate bowl to ensure all the dry ingredients are evenly distributed, then they can be added to the cake batter and folded in gently using a large metal spoon or plastic spatula. If using a table-top mixer, set it to the lowest speed. Finally, fold in the soaked fruits.

This very thick batter can now be added to the prepared tins. An ice cream scoop is a handy measure and can be plopped into each tin and divided evenly between the 9 tins without spills and splodges. No worries if you don't have one, a table-spoon is easy to manage.

I bake my Christmas cakes low and slow, then there is no need to 'feed' it with alcohol after baking as the cake is already moist and wholesome. Preheat the oven to 120°C/100°C fan/250°F/gas ½ and bake your mini cakes for 5½ hours. One large cake will take 10 hours. I usually put a large cake into the oven at 10pm and take it out at 8am the next day. The temperature of your oven is critical – even 10 degrees out will make a difference. If you are in any doubt about whether the cake is baked through, check with a temperature probe. The internal baked temperature needs to be 92–94°C (198–201°F).

Leave the cakes to go completely cold before carefully removing them from the tins. The mini cakes, along with their sleeve of lining paper, can be pushed from the tin using the end of a rolling pin, working from the blunt and ridged side of the tin.

I leave the baking paper on the cakes as it helps to keep

them moist, then wrap them in foil or another layer of grease-proof paper and place in a tin in a cool place until Christmas. My Christmas cake baking starts on 1 October, so it is one part of the Christmas shopping that can be done way ahead.

I have read many slow-cooker Christmas cake recipes and have tried baking my Christmas cake and small cakes in a slow cooker, but I have to say I am not a fan. I felt the finished cake, though baked through (internal temperature checked), was wet rather than moist and didn't have a baked feel or taste about it. I was pleased I tried, but I'll stick to the conventional oven.

HAND WARMERS

One of my favourite home-made gifts, and my family loved these tucked up in their hampers. Unlike the single-use, plastic-packaged alternatives, these are inexpensive and can be tossed into the compost when worn out.

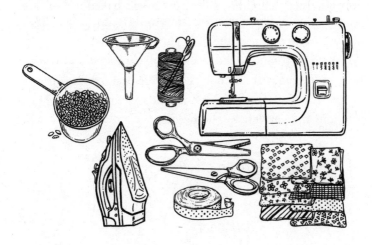

MAKES 1 PAIR OF WARMERS

You will need

> remnants of fabric – natural cotton or felted wool (no polyester or metal bits), to make 4 pieces each about 15 x 10cm (6 x 4in)
> pinking shears and scissors
> sewing machine or needle and cotton

funnel
iron
100g (3½oz) uncooked rice
ribbon to wrap into a pair

Cut the four pieces of fabric to size. Put the 'right' sides of pattern together, then using a sewing machine or by hand, stitch around all four sides, leaving a hole large enough to insert the pipe end of the funnel. Carefully turn the bag inside out, press with the iron, then simply fill with 100g (3½oz) uncooked rice and sew the hole closed by hand.

If sewing by hand I tend to use small back stitches to ensure those little grains of rice don't escape. A back stitch is easy to do and is as described; a stitch is made, then the needle goes back into the gap left by the needle.

Stitch about 1cm (½in) inside of the edge along three sides, fill with the rice, then holding the rice away from the opening, stitch along the fourth side.

If using felted wool, I prefer to stitch 'wrong' sides together, leaving the strong colour or pattern facing outwards, after first cutting out the shapes using pinking shears. This fabric doesn't fray and I like the cosy, warm feeling of felted wool. I actually picked up a pack of different-coloured squares, which were great for this job. The colours were plain, so if you're handy with embroidery thread, then each hand warmer can be personalized with initials!

I like to tie a couple of these hand warmers into pairs with a length of ribbon, an instruction tag and gift tag both cut from old birthday or Christmas cards.

To use

Place the hand warmers on the turntable and microwave for 30 seconds, then enjoy at least 30 minutes of cosy hands.

Bed Warmer

Cut the cost of getting cosy in bed. No electric blanket, no kettle boiling for a hot-water bottle, just a quick spin of the microwave before bed using minimal energy.

I was so delighted with my hand warmers that with a few modifications – slightly larger pieces of fabric – I went on to make bed warmers. The method is exactly the same as for the hand warmer above, though you may feel the bed warmer needs to be washed from time to time, so here a separate removable cover is included.

Imagine a piece of fabric the size of six hand warmers laid

side by side, because that is how I decided to design my bed warmer. Six individual pockets each containing 100g (3½oz) uncooked rice means that the rice remains evenly distributed (not falling to one end or the other) in the bed warmer, ensuring even heating and even warmth.

MAKES 1 BED WARMER

You will need

2 pieces of plain cotton fabric 45 x 30cm (18 x 12in) for the rice-filled warmer (an old sheet or pillowcase is perfect for this)
scissors or pinking shears
pins
pen, pencil or tailor's chalk and a ruler
sewing machine or needle and thread
funnel

600g (1lb 5oz) uncooked rice
2 pieces of cotton fabric or wool, 8 x 5½cm (20 x 14in) for the loose cover, plain or patterned
non-metal fasteners for the loose cover, or a 30cm (12in) strip of Velcro is easy to iron or sew on

Take the 2 cotton pieces for the rice-filled warmer, lay one over the other and pin together. Using the pencil, pen or chalk and ruler, mark out six even boxes, each 15 x 10cm (6 x 4in).

Machine or hand sew along each of the lines, leaving each pocket with a small hole at one end large enough to insert the pipe end of the funnel. One by one, fill each pocket with 100g

(3½oz) uncooked rice, then immediately seal the opening by hand or machine stitching. Continue until all six pockets are filled and the rice inside each pocket is free flowing.

The bed warmer part is made, so now make an attractive, slightly larger but simple cover so that the rice-filled pouch can be removed when necessary and the cover can be washed.

Pin the cover fabric right sides together and sew along the two long sides and one short side, leaving one short side open. Turn the bag inside out so the right sides are now facing you, then press with the iron, turn under the two open edges of the cover and press flat.

Fix the non-metal fasteners or iron or sew on the strip of Velcro fastening. The rice-filled inner pouch can be inserted into the cover, sealed and it is ready to use. Pop the bed warmer into the microwave for 90 seconds, snuggle up and sweet dreams!

MINT CREAMS

Home-made sweets don't come any easier or cheaper than Mint Creams. I use fresh egg white, though powdered egg white can be used instead if preferred. Follow the instructions on the pack to reconstitute, then use as fresh.

There is no cooking involved and this little treat can be decorated to suit the occasion. I use all types of small cutter for these, bearing in mind the mints need to be 5mm (¼in) thick. Dark chocolate always goes down well with mint, so let loose your artistic flair and decorate to your heart's content. They are great for gifts at Christmas, weddings, Easter – the list is endless. This is a home-made gift idea that the children can make and decorate. Get creative, I have made these as gifts with a Christmas pudding theme, or they would make wonderful wedding favours with a piped dinner jacket and bow tie detail. If you opt to use food colouring, pink mints look brilliant with white chocolate piping for a wedding dress. Start by piping the bodice top and dip in sparkly sprinkles while wet, then finish up on the rest of the dress detail.

MAKES 60

You will need

electric hand whisk
bowl
sieve
rolling pin

4cm (1½in) round cutter
baking sheet lined with baking paper
microwave-safe bowl or saucepan with a bowl that fits the
    top
wooden spoon
piping bag

1 egg white
3 tsp lemon juice
1 tsp peppermint extract
425g (15oz) icing sugar, sifted, plus extra for dusting
food colouring (optional)

FOR DECORATION
150g (6oz) dark chocolate, or a mix of dark and white
    chocolate if using food colouring
white sugar sprinkles

Using an electric hand whisk, whip up the egg white in a bowl
until stiff peaks form, add the lemon juice and peppermint
extract, then start to whisk in the icing sugar. The mixture
needs to be really thick, like the consistency of ready-to-roll
fondant.

The mixture will clog up your whisks, so use a knife to ease
it from the whisks. Finish by turning out the sugar ball onto
a surface dusted with icing sugar and kneading until smooth.
I divided my sugar into two and coloured one half a very pale
pink as I was making wedding sweets, though for Christmas
treats you may want to leave them snowy white and go to
town on the decorations instead.

Roll out the sugar paste to a thickness of 5mm (¼in), then

cut out with a 4cm (1½in) round cutter and transfer the mints onto a baking sheet covered in paper. Space them close together as you will have 60! Leave them to dry out in a cool but non-humid environment for about 3 hours or until they feel quite firm.

To decorate, for white mint creams melt the dark chocolate. You can do this in two ways. Place the chocolate, broken up, in a microwave-safe bowl in the microwave and melt in 30-second bursts, being careful not to overheat it or it will burn. It is better to melt it to a point where there are still a few solids in it. Give it a stir and you will find it will continue to melt on its own in a minute or two. Alternatively, place the chocolate pieces in a bowl set over a pan of hot water (not boiling), which is not touching the water. Stir regularly and the chocolate will soon melt.

Dip half of each mint cream into the melted chocolate. The chocolate needs to just coat the mint and not run off. If it is too warm and runny the chocolate will pool from the mint when you place it on the paper to dry. If this happens, leave the chocolate to cool and thicken a little, then try dipping again. The chocolate temperature needs to be around 30°C (86°F).

Once all the mints have a coating, transfer the remainder of the chocolate into a piping bag then cut the smallest hole in the end and pipe your decoration of choice.

For the decoration of coloured mints, melt the white chocolate as above and transfer to a piping bag and decorate as desired. Leave to cool and dry completely.

In an airtight tin these will keep for 3–4 weeks and can be gifted in a box, tin or pretty jar topped off with a paper, fabric or screw-on lid.

LUXURY DEEP-FILLED MINCE PIES

It may be that if you make your own mince pies you already have a favourite recipe. Maybe you make the pastry but prefer to buy the mincemeat, or it could be that for you the making of mince pies is a step too far with so much else to do at Christmas time.

I decided to include this recipe for these seasonal treats because of the little tips I use that make them less of a fiddle and faff at a time when there is so much other pressing Christmas prep.

A traditional treat, and I don't recall a single Christmas during my adult life when I have not made my own mince pies. Home baking is more tasty, cheaper and better for you than the factory processed alternatives, as you can control the sugar quantities, and these pies can be made well ahead (3 months ahead if you wish), to be baked from frozen as and when required – avoiding the need to dash out and be tempted by that last-minute, expensive impulse buy.

Rather than a traditional mincemeat that contains suet (either beef or veggie) and tends to bubble over in the oven, I have my own simple recipe mixed together in a pan then popped into jars, which can then be included as a hamper gift and/or spooned into bite-size mini or standard-sized mince pies.

Using cereal packet liners as an aid ensures the dough doesn't stick to the work surface, so no extra flour is required for rolling out, resulting in the pastry being the perfect balance of half fat to flour/sugar, and the finished baked goods are absolutely perfect and mouth-watering, not hard due to the dough being overworked with excess flour added.

An upcycled cereal packet liner is so handy. Use it to wrap foods for the fridge or freezer, roll out pastry and then cut into strips to get ahead with your prep for mince pie baking (see page 294). They keep sticky labels alive, too! A follower told me she invested in Christmas-themed window stickers each year, then at the end of the festive period would peel them off and throw them away. By peeling off and sticking them to a used cereal packet liner, then storing away with the other decorations, she can now reuse them!

MAKES 12–18 PIES (DEPENDING ON
THE STYLE AND CUTTERS USED)

You will need

large mixing bowl
fine grater
wooden spoon or spatula
large saucepan
food processor (but can be made by hand)
2 cereal packet liners (pulled apart to make two single food-grade plastic sheets) or 2 large freezer bags each cut down one side and across the bottom
round-bladed knife
clean sterilized jars (see page 223 for sterilizing methods)
rolling pin
9cm (3½in) (base), 7cm (2¾in) (lid) fluted pastry cutters and/or snowflake fondant cutter for a lighter option
2 x 12-hole deep muffin tins

FOR THE MINCEMEAT

300g (10½oz) mixed fruit and peel

100g (3½oz) dried apricots, chopped into raisin-sized pieces

100g (3½oz) dried cranberries

½ tsp ground mace or grated nutmeg

1 tsp ground cinnamon

2 tsp ground mixed spice

6 cardamom pods, split and the seeds crushed

6 tbsp Cointreau/brandy/port or a mixture

finely grated zest of 1 orange and 1 lemon

50g (1¾oz) butter

200g (7oz) soft brown sugar

8 tbsp orange and lemon juice from the fruits

FOR THE PASTRY

400g pastry (see page 184), replacing 1oz flour for icing sugar

1oz icing sugar, plus extra for dusting

lining paste (see page 16, optional)

First make the mincemeat. Place the fruits, spices and alcohol in a large mixing bowl. Finely grate the zests from the orange and the lemon and add these to the bowl of fruit, then give everything a good stir. In a large pan melt the butter, the sugar and the fruit juices over a low heat. When the sugar is no longer grainy add all the other ingredients, making sure everything is well combined. Stir over a low–medium heat then bring to boil and simmer for 10 minutes. Take from the heat, allow to cool slightly, then transfer to warm sterilized jars and seal. If you want to use the mincemeat straight away, make sure it is cold.

Now make a quantity of pastry (see page 184), remembering

to replace 1oz flour for 1oz icing sugar for this recipe, adding the icing sugar in with the flour.

If using a mixer, gently remove it from the mixer and shape into a ball, then wrap in a sheet of cereal packet liner and chill for half an hour.

If making the pastry by hand, bring together with your hands and wrap and chill as for machine-mixed pastry.

Once the pastry dough has firmed up, place the ball between the two sheets of liner and begin to roll out the pastry to a thickness of a £1 coin. Cut out 12 circles with a 9cm (3½in) pastry cutter for the bases along with 12 x 7cm (2¾in) lids.

||||||||||||||||||||||||||||||||||||||||||||||||||||||||||||||||||||||||||||||||||||||||||||||||||||||||

TIP: For a lighter, 'less-pastry' option – and my favourite – use a fondant snowflake cutter. These are widely available and can be used to cut out pastry, though make sure the dough is well chilled and the cutter is floured first.

||||||||||||||||||||||||||||||||||||||||||||||||||||||||||||||||||||||||||||||||||||||||||||||||||||||||

When it comes to cutting out, peel off one sheet of plastic and cut out the circles with the dough still stuck to the base sheet, then peel them off. If at any time the dough begins to stick to the plastic or leave any residue, simply pop the sheet into the fridge for 10 minutes or so.

Once all of the cutting out is done, having rerolled and reused the pastry trimmings, grease the muffin tins with butter or lining paste and line with the pastry bases. How many times have you tried to line a deep muffin tin with pastry only to put your fingers through it? To avoid this, lay the pastry base over the hole in the tin, then using the end of your rolling pin gently ease the pastry into the base of the tin. Hands-free and no splitting.

Once the bases are in place, fill with the mincemeat. Add 2–3 teaspoons mincemeat to each cup or sufficient to come almost to the top, gently firming it down with the back of a teaspoon. Simply lay over the lids, if using, or the snowflake cutout – do not squash it down. There's no need to dampen the edges of the pastry, or to egg-wash the mince pies, as there is enough sugar in the pastry to colour them.

Chill until the oven comes to temperature, then bake at 200°C/180°C fan/400°F/gas 6 for 15–18 minutes until the mince pies are light golden. Allow to cool before removing them from the muffin tin.

To remove from the tin without the need to dig them out with a knife, lay a clean tea towel over the cooled mince pies, place an inverted cooling rack over them and quickly flip. Lift off the tin – the upside-down mince pies will be turned out onto the tea towel, then they can be quickly turned the right way and given the final beauty treatment with a dusting of icing sugar.

TIP: To get ahead I often make mince pies and freeze them unbaked. Do not grease the muffin tin but instead line with strips (about 1cm (½in) wide) of cereal packet liner. Greaseproof paper I have found is not robust enough, whereas this upcycled food-grade plastic is. Lay a long strip of the liner over the top of three cups of the tin. Hold onto one end and gently ease the pastry base into the first cup using the end of the rolling pin as described. Repeat, holding onto one end of the liner as you go. Once fully assembled, pop the pies in the freezer for 10–15 minutes to firm up. Take from the freezer then pull on one end of the strip, which will flip the pies out of the tin. The unbaked pies are sturdy and firm and can be packed into a box then put back into the freezer. When ready to bake, take from the freezer – there's no need to thaw, I bake them from frozen. Simply brush the original muffin tin with lining paste, pop the filled frozen pie into the cup, pop straight into the oven and add 5 minutes to the baking time. Leave to cool in the tin before turning out. To turn them out effortlessly, lay a clean tea towel over the tray then invert a cooling rack, place on top of the tea towel and flip the whole lot over. The cooled pies will leave the tin without any problem. It is so handy to have these 'ready to bake' mince pies – bake as many or as few as you need and it's one job less to do right on Christmas.

CRANBERRIES

Fresh seasonal cranberries hit the shelves in early December, and as soon as I see packs of these shiny beauties I grab one or two. People refer to cranberries as a superfood because they contain all kinds of health-boosting benefits. When I did a quick internet search cranberries are definitely up there, but if you have ever tasted fresh cranberries you will know them as hard, bitter, inedible bullets. However, with a little gentle TLC we can transform them into soft, juicy sweet berries that retain their perfect shape without splitting. A natural Christmas treat that will decorate your festive cakes, desserts and trifles, or you can just eat them on their own. I set aside a few cranberries before making my cranberry sauce, below.

You will need

small microwave-safe bowl
small heatproof bowl and plate to cover
small saucepan to fit the bowl

100g (3½oz) sugar, plus 1–2 tbsp
2 tbsp water
50g (1¾oz) cranberries

Add the 100g (3½oz) sugar and the water to a small microwave-safe bowl and microwave for a minute or so until you see the sugar has dissolved. Add the raw cranberries, cover with a plate and pop into the microwave at 10 per cent power (100 watts) for just 5 minutes. Leave covered over-night.

For those without a microwave, dissolve the sugar and water in a bowl set over a pan of simmering water. Add the cranberries, stir, then cover with a lid or plate. Simmer for 5 minutes then turn the heat off but leave the pan and bowl in place overnight.

Next day, drain on absorbent paper before tossing in 1–2 tablespoons of caster sugar.

Keep the cranberries in an airtight container for 4–5 days.

Cranberry Sauce

A suitable hamper gift or a brilliant dish to bring offer to bring to any festive meal. Lots of people like to divide the cooking and baking chores at Christmas, not only is it less work for the cook but everyone gets the chance to show off their favourite recipe. If, however, you feel you haven't the confidence, expertise or know-how to compete with those in the group who seem to always manage to pull off something amazing, offer to bring the cranberry sauce! It's a winner.

When around the table there are lots of oohs and aahs about the taste, you can remind them that you've made it using fresh cranberries and that you always make your own, it's head and shoulders above bought, containing less sugar, even though it may be a little more expensive.

You will need

for oven cooking: ovenproof casserole with a well-fitting lid

for stove top or hob cooking: large, roomy, deep-sided
    frying pan
for slow cooker: use proprietary bowl
for microwave: deep non-metal dish or casserole with a lid
wooden spoon
fork
2 x 1lb (500g) clean jars with lids

300g (10½oz) fresh cranberries
zest of 1 orange
120g (4¼oz) caster sugar
2 tbsp Cointreau, or orange juice for an alcohol-free version

Add the cranberries, orange zest and juice, or Cointreau, into the casserole pan. Top with the sugar, stir, then pop the lid on and cook at 200°C/180°C fan/400°F/gas 6 for 30 minutes. This recipe can also be made in a saucepan on the stove top, in the microwave or in a slow cooker.

Timings are easy to calculate – as soon as the cranberries are soft, the sauce is done. I would suggest 2 hours in a slow cooker, 4–5 minutes in the microwave and around 20–25 minutes on the hob. Popping it in the oven when something else is in there is the one that works for me.

Once cooked, take out of the oven, remove the lid, mash gently with a fork, cool and taste. If it's not sweet enough for you, add a little more sugar. Transfer to a serving bowl to use straight away (served at room temperature) or transfer into jars where it will keep for at least 6 weeks in the fridge, though I have never put it to the full 'use-by' test because there are rarely any leftovers.

SPRAY PAINTING

For many craft projects, spray paint is often used. Every year I make a compostable Christmas wreath, but before I went green I used to buy cans of expensive aerosol spray paints. I would add a layer of sprayed bling to pine cones, evergreens, dried grasses, seed heads, interesting twigs and branches. I now understand that as well as being harmful to the environment, and particularly the ozone layer, aerosol spray paints give off harmful fumes and the cans themselves are difficult to dispose of. It also increased the cost of my wreath!

By spraying my natural foraged items, I was making them no longer suitable for composting. I had to think of something that was cheaper than spray paint, that would be degradable but would give me some bling or a coloured finish to my bio-degradable Christmas decorations.

This recipe will make about 70ml (2½oz) of spray paint, which I find is sufficient for one colour.

You will need

digital weighing scales
small bowl and spoon
funnel
spray bottle

30g (1oz) cornflour
40ml (1½fl oz) cold water
food or soap colour

edible glitter (optional, mine had gone past its 'use-by' so was no longer considered edible, which is a great biodegradable upcycle for this job)

Weigh the cornflour into a small bowl and gradually stir in the cold water to make a thin paste, then add your colour of choice. I leave mine white for a simple 'frosted' look on dried grasses, teasels, pine cones, etc. Use the funnel to transfer to a recycled spray bottle.

To use, make sure the items to be coloured are dry to the touch, then spray. I try to do this outside or in the shed but if it is necessary to spray indoors then cover work surfaces with sheets of newspaper as the overspray will settle itself everywhere.

I used a dark red to spray hydrangea heads – they looked amazing – then sprinkled them with red edible glitter. My seedheads, teasels and pine cones I sprayed white then sprinkled over silver edible glitter.

I can't tell you how happy this made me, knowing I could simply toss the whole lot into the compost bin when the festivities were over. Use for wreath-making, table decorations or a decorative winter display inside the house.

Conclusion

I have thoroughly enjoyed the writing of this book and I sincerely hope you have enjoyed the reading too.

Have a go at my recipes, feel confident to tackle even the most difficult of laundry stains with gusto, then go further and rescue items that maybe would otherwise have ended their days prematurely. Day by day you will adopt a new positive attitude to even the most challenging of household tasks.

Let us feel armed, excited and equipped to meet head head-on the budget and climate pressures that face us day in and day out and will no doubt go on to challenge future generations. We know the pressures are not going to go away, but with a growing knowledge and confidence I know that we can make a huge difference.

Our money can and will go further, our food waste can be less – and our use of valuable energy as a consequence of our lifestyle change is going to be drastically reduced. As I write the last few lines of this, my fifth book – it is by no means the end of my green journey – 'upwards and onwards', I say.

I hope you will join me as we continue to mix our own, make our own and generally get on and do things for ourselves.

Information is power and if we have the facts, budget recipes (cleaning, cooking and baking) and know how to handle daily snags, we can sort out many problems. Our efforts come together to make a big difference to our household budgets, and our greener actions and choices ultimately protect our precious planet.

Acknowledgements

This book has been a joy to write, plan and structure and I am excited as I realise more and more people want to embrace a green way of living yet being mindful that for something to really work, it has to be done in a cost conscious way.

As always, there are a group of people around me that I have to thank because without them my thoughts, aspirations, experiences and green plans would not have materialised.

My publisher, Pan Macmillan, and importantly, Hockley, who has always been there to keep me on track, my agent and friends at Yellow Poppy Media who for many years now have kept me going and always encouraged and supported my work.

My followers and you the readers, of course, because without your engagement, interest and feedback I wouldn't be here writing the fourth of this gorgeous set of books.

On a personal level of course there are my family members and close friends who know me better than I know myself and last and by no means least 'him indoors' who continues to just be there. Tim has that ability to never lose sight of what is important in life. He takes away the stresses, carries the bags, packs the car, upgrades computers, phones and devices, manages the paperwork - leaving me to quietly get on and do what I do.

Thanks everyone!

Author biography

Nancy Birtwhistle is a *Sunday Times* best-selling author, lifelong gardener and Hull-born baker who won the fifth series of *The Great British Bake Off* in 2014. Motivated by protecting the planet for her ten grandchildren, Nancy decided to change how she used plastic, single-use products and chemicals in her home. Sharing her tips online, she amassed an engaged international following of devoted fans interested not only in her delicious recipes, but also her innovative ideas and time-saving swaps that rethink everyday house and garden tasks to make as little impact on the environment as possible. Nancy worked as a GP practice manager in the NHS for thirty-six years until she retired in 2007. She lives in Lincolnshire with her husband, dogs and rescue hens.

Connect with Nancy on Instagram: @nancy.birtwhistle, on X: @nancybbakes, on TikTok: @nancy_birtwhistle, or through her website: nancybirtwhistle.co.uk.

Portrait by Mel Four.

Index

coloured washing 19–20, 63
  colour run 65–6
condensation 25, 27, 105–6
containers, removing stains and
  odours 93
cornflour: egg-free custard 194–5
  spray paint 298–9
cranberries 295–7
  cranberry sauce 296–7
  luxury deep-filled mince pies
  289–94
crazed porcelain 42–3
cream 152
  homemade butter 211–13
  no-churn 'budget' creamy ice
  cream 226–7
  strawberry cups 190–3
cream cleaner 14–15
  cleaning stone and slate 109–10
  hand cleaner 148
  mould on wood 30–1
crème pâtissière 224–5
  no-churn 'budget' creamy ice
  cream 226–7
  strawberry cups 190–3
crisps 238–9
  carrot crisps 204
crockery, stuck-fast 90
cupcake cases 162–3
curry stains 61, 69–70, 93
curtains, mouldy 25, 27, 28–30, 105
custard, egg-free 194–5

D
darning 131–4
de-icer 142–3
detergent 48
  liquid detergent 52–4
  powder detergent 58–9

travel wash 55–7
diarrhoea stains 35–7, 56–7
dirt 63
dishwashers, eradicating smells
  111–14
dresses, dry-clean-only 79
dried fruit: Christmas cake
  276–80
  dried citrus slices 234–5
  luxury deep-filled mince pies
  289–94

E
egg-free custard 194–5
eggs: crème pâtissière 224–5
  freezing 152
  minute lemon curd 221–2
  poached eggs 228–9
  scrambled eggs 232–3
  soft- and hard-boiled eggs
  230–1
energy consumption 7–11, 242
Epsom salts: powder detergent
  58–9
evaporated milk: flexi rice
  pudding 257–60
Eve's Pudding, mock 179–81

F
fabrics: fixing scorches 20
  mould on 27–30
fatty stains 62
filters, cleaning 112, 114
fireplaces: cleaning glass door
  fronts 107–8
  stone and slate hearths 109–10
flannels, washing 73–4
flapjacks, cherry and coconut
  199–201

mint creams 286–8
mites, flour 99
mock Eve's Pudding 179–81
moisture: home-made moisture
    absorber 25–6
    steamy windows 105–6
mould 23–34
    on bread 128, 173
    on fabrics 27–30
    on leather bags and shoes 31–2
    moisture absorber 25–6
    permanent mould stains 33–4
    on walls, paintwork and
        wallpaper 24–6
    in washing machines 113
    on wood 30–1
mousse, chocolate 248–52
mud 38–9, 63
muffins: chocolate chip muffins 165
    crunchy lemon drizzle muffins
        166
    cupcake cases 162–3
    raspberry and almond muffins
        163–5
mushroom risotto 243–7

N
no-churn 'budget' creamy ice
    cream 226–7
nuts: high-energy/low-energy
    'no-bake' bars 202–3

O
oats: cherry and coconut flapjack
    199–201
    high-energy/low-energy
        'no-bake' bars 202–3
odours: flasks and storage
    containers 91–3

laundry 63
    second-hand clothes and
        furniture 78–80
    stinky spills 35–7
    washing machines and
        dishwashers 111–14
oils: expired 101
    reusing cooking oil 99–100
olive oil: simple strawberry
    vinaigrette 168
onions, chopping finely 158–9
oranges: award-winning
    marmalade 271–5
    dried citrus slices 234–5
    rhubarb, orange and ginger
        Eve's Pudding 179–81
ovens 8, 9, 160

P
paint: mouldy paintwork 24–6
    stains 63, 67–8, 118–20
pans: burnt pans 85–7
    renewing and reviving cast iron
        pans 88–9
pasta salad 236–7
pastry tips 184–93
    jam and lemon curd tarts
        187–9
    luxury deep-filled mince pies
        289–94
    pastry dough 185–6
    strawberry cups 190–3
pets: stains 35–7, 39
    travel wash 56–7
pies: luxury deep-filled mince pies
    289–94
    pie fillings 209–10
pillows, cleaning 81–2
pizza, 'pretend' 174–5

Notes

Also by Nancy Birtwhistle

Looking to clean up your act when it comes to looking after your home?

'Nancy's enthusiasm and energy shine through . . . I have learned loads from this book!'
Aggie MacKenzie, co-presenter, Channel 4's *How Clean is Your House?*

'From baking, to gardening, to organization, resourcefulness, and just her incredible energy . . . she creates art out of everything in her life, and takes so much joy in the process.'
Jonathan Van Ness, *Queer Eye*

AVAILABLE NOW